Quakerism in Lincolnshire

An informal history

Susan Davies

YARD PUBLISHING SERVICES
1989

© 1989 Susan E. A. Davies
ISBN 0 9514910 0 8

First published in 1989 by Yard Publishing Services
11 Minster Yard,
Lincoln, LN2 1PJ

Reprinted 2007 by The Religious Society of Friends (Quakers)

Printed by G. W. Belton Ltd, Heaton Street, Gainsborough

British Library Davies, Cataloguing in Publication Data
Davies, Susan, *1921-*
Quakerism in Lincolnshire.
1. Lincolnshire. Quakers, history
I. Title
289.6'425'3

ISBN 0-9514910-0-8

Quakerism
in
Lincolnshire

The quest for truth is itself a prayer by being a reaching out of the human spirit toward a fuller perception and absorption of what it lacks.

I BELIEVE IN MAN
Lord Sorenson 1970

A RECORD

Wherein are Severall writings containing wholesome Advice to the Quarterly and Monthly Meetings.

HEREIN ALSO ARE RECORDED

The Sufferings of the People of God (called Quakers) in Lincolnshire Jnflicted vppon them for Righteousnes sake Since the Eighth Month in the yeare One Thousand six Hundred Fifty Foure. At which Time God did visit vs with the Day spring from on High, and gaue vs to beleiue in the Light of his Eternall Son Christ Jesus, and also to Suffer for his Name sake To whom over all be Glory & Dominion for Ever, because hee hath strengthened vs to suffer both Reproaches Stoneings and Buffetings, the Spoiling of our Goods, Bonds & Jmprisonments, as this Following Record will make manifest, Wherein the Names of the sufferers with the true & Reall Cause of their sufferings are faithfully set downe, As alfe the time of their Sufferings, and by whom they were Persecuted as neare as can be Gathered, From the Relation of the sufferers themselues, & those that haue bene eie witnesses of their sufferings and Simpathized with them, therein.

Here is also A Memoriall of things

Worthy the Knowledge of Posterity Done by Friends at their Quarterly Meetings &c

Title page of seventeenth-century Quaker Book of Records. By courtesy of Lincolnshire Archives Office

CONTENTS

ACKNOWLEDGEMENTS

During the writing of this history I have received encouragement and support from the Friends of Lincoln Meeting and Lincolnshire Monthly Meeting, and I thank them and, in particular, Joyce Pritchard for sharing with me their memories of late Friends and of events connected with the Meetings in Lincolnshire. I am indebted to Edward H. Milligan and Gerald A. J. Hodgett of the Friends' Historical Society and to Dr Dennis and Mrs Joan Mills for their helpful suggestions and advice. For their always courteous help I thank the staff of Friends Library, London, the staffs of the Lincoln Lending Library and Lincoln Reference Library, and the archivists and staff of Lincolnshire Archives Office for their kind attention over a period of many months.

I would like to thank all those who have allowed me to use their photographs. They are acknowledged individually in the captions.

I also wish to acknowledge the assistance of Elizabeth Nurser and Penny Fogg of Yard Publishing Services in the preparation of the book. Max Marschner of Ampersand Designs was responsible for the design of the cover.

Finally, for help towards publication costs, thanks are extended gratefully to Alfred and Jean Youngs for their generosity.

Susan Davies
Lincoln
June 1989

FOREWORD

The writing of this history is to commemorate the tercentenary of the building of the Friends' Meeting House, Lincoln. The main aim of the work has been to present to new Friends and attenders an informal introduction to the history of Quakerism in Lincolnshire.

Lincoln Meeting House has the distinction of being the first licensed non-conformist place of worship in the city of Lincoln. It was built in 1689, the year of the Toleration Act, being constructed in the vernacular design of that age and although the outward appearance is unpretentious its interior still retains many of the original features. It has been described by Niklaus Pevsner '...as the most impressive non-conformist structure in Lincoln...'

The story of Quakerism in Lincolnshire started 40 years before the Meeting House was built, and it is also a history in which past Friends have been able to 'speak for themselves', because it is their own accounts, taken from the Records and Minute Books of their Meetings during the past 339 years, that have been drawn upon extensively.

This work is dedicated to all those Friends who, in the past, set out on their spiritual journeys, despite the hazards, adventurously and cheerfully. It is dedicated to our present Friends who, at this time, are witnessing rapid technological change and standing prayerfully on the brink of a Space Age. And, it is dedicated to our future Friends: God bless and keep them, their world, and its natural environments safe.

Although the history is informal it is hoped that it will act as a foundation for Friends and students wishing to carry out further detailed research into individual Quaker families and Lincolnshire Meetings and also that it may be of some help to local and family historians.

Footnotes have not been used. At the back of the book there is a relevant list of the historical sources used and quoted from and a bibliography of works from which was obtained further useful information.

Susan E. A. Davies
Lincoln Meeting, 1989
Lincolnshire Monthly Meeting, 1989

WHO ARE THE QUAKERS?

Quakerism began in the seventeenth century – a period when authority was questioned and opinions were often polarised. In the deeply divided society during the Civil War religion was of passionate interest. It was then that a group of men and women including George Fox (1624–1691) came together to revive what they saw as 'primitive Christianity'. They could not accept that the forms of Christianity that they observed around them were in keeping with the teachings of Jesus.

George Fox's long and painful searching for truth was rewarded by a sudden conviction that God was immediately accessible to each individual. At the point of despair, he writes, 'Then, oh then, I heard a voice which said, "There is one, even Christ Jesus, that can speak to thy condition", and when I heard it my heart did leap for joy.'

This was the seed of Quakerism. The soil was ready in the Midlands, Yorkshire and north-west England, where there were groups seeking a way to live more simply and truly the Christian life. He united many of the scattered groups into what has become the Religious Society of Friends.

Many of the early Quakers were persecuted. Meetings for worship were often broken up. Thousands were heavily fined and many were imprisoned before the right to freedom of worship was finally won for dissenters. The struggle for tolerance led Quakers to see how they themselves might help to lessen the harshness of oppression existing within and between nations.

The meeting for worship is at the centre of Quaker life. It begins as Quakers sit in the meeting room, gathering together in a silence that grows deeper as it progresses. Here they open themselves to the love of God and to that of God in each other.

The meeting house is simple. There are no ornaments or religious symbols. Neither is there an appointed minister or pastor. The responsibility of the meeting belongs to all. Anyone may speak when he or she is called to do so; this is known as vocal ministry. These meetings are open to all and visitors are particularly welcome. The word 'meeting' refers both to the activity and to the group of worshippers.

An extract from WHO ARE THE QUAKERS?, a leaflet issued in 1986 by the Quaker Home Service.

AN OVERVIEW

The devolution of Monthly Meetings in Lincolnshire from 1667 to 1920

All dates before 14 September 1752 are in the 'Old Style' when the Julian Calendar was still in use. The present calendar, devised by Gregory XIII, was introduced into the United Kingdom on 3 September when that date then became the 14th of September. Up to that time 25 March had been reckoned as the first day of the first month of a new year.

Separate or Particular Meetings for Worship were held in towns and villages. Representatives from these Meetings attended Monthly Business Meetings. Representatives from each Monthly Meeting attended four Quarterly and one Yearly Meeting.

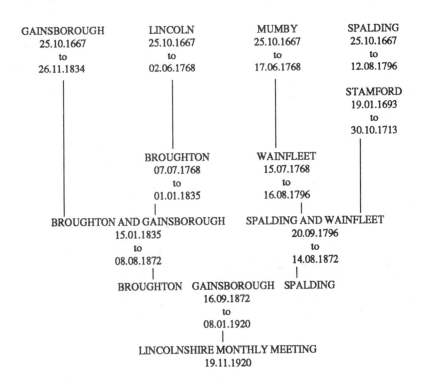

GAINSBOROUGH
25.10.1667
to
26.11.1834

LINCOLN
25.10.1667
to
02.06.1768

MUMBY
25.10.1667
to
17.06.1768

SPALDING
25.10.1667
to
12.08.1796

STAMFORD
19.01.1693
to
30.10.1713

BROUGHTON
07.07.1768
to
01.01.1835

WAINFLEET
15.07.1768
to
16.08.1796

BROUGHTON AND GAINSBOROUGH
15.01.1835
to
08.08.1872

SPALDING AND WAINFLEET
20.09.1796
to
14.08.1872

BROUGHTON GAINSBOROUGH SPALDING
16.09.1872
to
08.01.1920

LINCOLNSHIRE MONTHLY MEETING
19.11.1920

Religious toleration denied 1559-1689

After the upheaval of the English Reformation it was established in the reign of Queen Elizabeth I that the religion of the State should avoid the extremes of Roman Catholicism and of Protestant Calvinism. In 1559 an Act of Uniformity was passed and this meant that all must conform to the beliefs and practices laid down in the then established Prayer Book. This was found unacceptable by some and by the early seventeenth century there were dissenting groups of Presbyterians, Baptists and other independent congregations which were meeting for worship illegally.

During the Civil War and Interregnum many Protestant dissenting sects gained a certain amount of freedom to worship, but individuals were often prosecuted on civil charges or for being suspected of political subversion.

In 1660 Charles II was restored to the throne and a religious uniformity towards a Protestant Anglican State Church was re-established as a defence against revolution. Several penal laws were introduced and dissenters lost both civic and religious rights. Under these laws members of all denominations suffered persecution; almost 2000 ministers were ejected from their livings and dissenters were fined and imprisoned, with many dying in the prisons.

Limited toleration granted 1689

The succession to the throne of James II in 1685 brought the fear that the king's leaning towards Roman Catholicism would bring about civil unrest, and in 1688 the king was forced into exile. The king's Protestant daughter, Mary, and her husband William of Orange were installed on the throne and a Toleration Act was passed in May 1689 which gave a limited toleration to those Protestant dissenters who had supported the change of government.

The Toleration Act did not apply to Unitarians or to Roman Catholics, nor did it apply to those dissenters who were unable to subscribe to most of the Thirty-nine Articles of the Anglican Church. Meeting places for worship had to apply for and be granted a licence at the discretion of the authorities. Dissenters were not admitted to the Universities.

A refusal to pay tithes and a refusal to swear on oath was still punishable and dissenters were still not allowed to hold public offices.

Toleration extended (some landmarks)

1779   Dissenting ministers no longer had to subscribe to the Thirty-Nine Articles.
1791   Roman Catholics allowed to hold some public offices but not to sit as MPs or to worship in their own places of worship.
1813   The privileges extended to Unitarians.
1828   Dissenters allowed to hold most public offices.
1829   Roman Catholics allowed to own property and to become MPs.
1855   Registration and protection extended to all religious groups.
1858   Jews allowed to own property and to become MPs.
1871   Religious tests abolished for entry into the Universities of Oxford, Cambridge and Durham.
1880   The right of a non-conformist to be buried in a Church of England graveyard without a Church of England service.

A brief summary of the charge of tithes upon the community towards the maintenance of the clergy and for church purposes

The *Great Tithe* or *Rectorial Tithe*. and the *Small Tithe* or *Vicarial Tithe where the rector and the incumbent were different people.*
These were obtained from
1.   The Praedine Tithe which came from one tenth of the main produce of the land, for example, corn, oats and wood.
2.   The Mixed Tithe came from one tenth of stock and labour.
3.   The Personal Tithe was allocated from one tenth part of the profits of labour.

The private incomes and personal property of the clergy varied and in 1704 Queen Anne surrendered money from taxes which had been inherited in the past by the Crown from the Pope. This was formed into a fund 'Queen Anne's Bounty' for the use of poor incumbents and which helped to raise their status. In 1836 the Tithe Commutation Act meant that a rent charge was based upon the price of corn. In 1925 the Tithe Act abolished this rent charge. In 1936 the Tithe Act changed Queen Anne's Bounty to Government Stock.

Distribution of Quakerism in Lincolnshire

Before 1689 dissenting sects met in houses that were unlicensed for Meetings for Worship; they were therefore liable to be arrested. From an analysis of existing Quaker records and Business Meetings Minutes and from accounts of where Friends were arrested whilst attending Meetings for Worship, and from a scrutiny of the wills of Friends and the deeds of Quaker properties, it has been possible to show some of the many villages and towns where Friends lived and met during and after the first forty years of Quakerism in Lincolnshire.

. The boundaries of the four Monthly Meetings, Lincoln, Gainsborough, Mumby and Spalding are shown below. The dots show where Friends met to worship and from where representatives came when George Fox visited Lincoln on 25 December 1667 in order to set up the Monthly Business Meetings. The ringed dots are the places shown in capitals where Friends met to hold those Monthly Meetings.

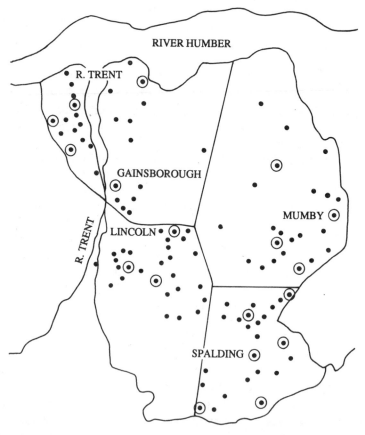

Distribution of communities of Friends c. 1667. Drawn by J. Peacock.

Lincoln	Gainsborough	Mumby	Spalding
LINCOLN	GAINSBOROUGH	MUMBY	SPALDING
Bracebridge Heath	Lea	Hogsthorpe	Long Sutton
Skellingthorpe	Burton	Hagnaby	GEDNEY
South Hykeham	Marton	Huttoft	Weston
Fiskerton	Marton	Spilsby	Moulton
Waddington	Willingham	Anderby	Whaplode
Harmston	HAXEY	Asterby	Cowbit
Navenby	Epworth	Partney Mills	BOSTON
Nocton	GARTHORPE	Somercotes	Wyberton
Sutton	CROWLE	LEAKE	Frampton
Claypole	Belton	Wrangle	Donington
Stapleford	Beltoft	Fishtoft	BICKER
BECKINGHAM	Butterwick	Wainfleet	Swineshead
FULBECK	Yealand	BINBROOK	Kirton
Honington	Fockerby	Raithby	Wigtoft
Ancaster	Adlingfleet	Barnoldby	Hale
Leasingham	Ousefleet	Tealby	Helpringham
Willoughby	Luddington	TUNBY	Stamford
Welby	Amcotts	Tattershall	Tallington
Welbourn	WINTERINGHAM	Revesby	Deeping
Leadenham	Alkborough	Mareham	CROWLAND
Sleaford	Roxby	Ashby	Careby
Norton Disney	Thealby	Wootten	Thurlby
Barnby le Willows	Whitton	Gautby	
Brant Broughton	Appleby		
Swinderby	Brigg		
Manthorpe	Glentworth		
Grantham			

After the Toleration Act May 1689

By September 1689 seven houses in Lincolnshire had been granted licences for Meeting for Worship. They were at Fulbeck, West Willoughby, Manthorpe, Post Witham, Careby, Swinderby and Thurlby. Since that date, over the years, there have been licensed Meeting Houses at

Lincoln	Gainsborough	Spalding	Mumby	Grimsby
Beckingham	Beltoft	Gedney	Tumby W'dside	Brigg
Navenby	Winteringham	Boston	Wainfleet	Scunthorpe
Waddington	West Butterwick	Stamford	Sturton	Leake
Bourne	Brant Broughton	Epworth	Swineshead	Thealby

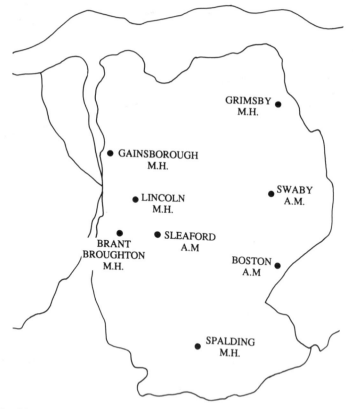

The five Meeting Houses for Worship in 1989 and the three allowed Meetings for Worship at Boston, Sleaford and Swaby. Drawn by J. Peacock.

Chapter 1

ON BOTH SIDES OF THE TRENT

After this I came to Balby, from whence several Friends went with me into Lincolnshire, where I had formerly been, some went to the steeple-houses, and some to the Separate meetings. There came to the meeting where I was the sheriff of Lincoln, and several with him. And he made a great contention and a jangling for a time, but at length the Lord's power struck him, that he was convinced of the truth, and received the word of life, as did several others also that had opposed, and continued amongst Friends until they died. Great meetings there were, and a large convincement in those parts and many were turned to the Lord...And there came one Sir Richard Wray, and he was convinced, and his brother and his brother's wife, who died in the Truth, though he afterwards run out, and after I had visited these counties I came into Derbyshire; the sheriff of Lincoln, who was lately convinced, being with me... *(The Journal of George Fox*, Nickalls Edition, Ch. 5, p. 180.)

Two of the Friends with George Fox on that particular journey were George Whitehead and Alexander Parker; the journey was made in 1654 and it is from an account by Alexander Parker of the same journey that we also learn that the approach into Lincolnshire was made on foot. George Fox was then a young man of about 30 years of age and news of his preaching had reached into many parts of the county since he had made his first visits to the area. From 1647 onwards, during his journeys throughout England, he had met groups of Baptists and Separatist religious sects of all persuasions on both side of the Trent, where he preached to gathered meetings of people known as 'Children of the Light'. His appearance in Gainsborough in 1651 had caused an uproar in the town. It had been on one of those journeys, on 30 October 1650 at Derby, that he and his companions had been brought before Justice Gervase Bennett and charged with blasphemy: this had resulted in an imprisonment which had lasted for nearly a year. However, there is some evidence that it was also the occasion when Friends acquired the name Quaker. Quaking during a religious meeting was not unknown during those times, it being generated by the enthusiasm and religious fervour of many of the dissenting sects. Nevertheless, George Fox's own account in his Journal states that Justice Bennett gave the name to Friends because Fox had bidden the

1

magistrate to 'tremble at the name of the Lord'. It seems that it was soon after that incident that 'Quaker' was in general use when alluding to Friends, as is shown by a paper written by George Fox to the authorities from a dungeon in Carlisle in 1653: 'To that of God in your consciences I speak; declare or write your dissatisfaction to any of them whom you call Quakers, that Truth may be exalted...'

However, in those early days Friends were known amongst themselves as 'Friends of Truth'.

The men and women of Lincolnshire who met and heard George Fox from 1648 onwards were people whose lives had been shaken by the turmoil of the Civil War and by the ferment caused by the upsurge of changing religious and political ideas at that time. George Fox's stated belief that God and the Spirit of Christ dwelt in the hearts and minds of men and women – that 'there was that of God in every one' – echoed for some of his listeners their already formed religious thinking and for others, like the sheriff of Lincoln, it was to lead to a dramatic change in their lives.

That there were many ready and eager listeners to his message can be understood when it it learned that in Lincolnshire, as in many other parts of the country, there had been strong religious dissension amongst both the clerics and the laity throughout the previous century. At the beginning of the century, in 1604, 61 ministers in Lincolnshire were rebuked for not conforming strictly to the Book of Common Prayer. Harold Brace, in the foreword of his compilation of the Minutes of Gainsborough Friends' Monthly Meetings, states '...that as early as 1585 John Huddlestone, vicar of Saxilby, was amongst those local clergy in the County of Lincoln, who were suspended for not wearing the surplice.'

The dissension increased during the controversial reigns of James I and his son Charles I and many puritan clergy and dissenters in the area had endured persecution during Archbishop Laud's domination over ecclesiastical and political affairs during the reign of Charles. The Bishop of Lincoln, John Williams, had not escaped Laud's wrath and had been accused of favouring puritans and nonconformists, whilst in 1630, after a long-standing personal feud between the two, John Williams was suspended from office and imprisoned in the Tower of London, where he was held until 1640. The demands for payment of tithes and a laxity towards the care of their parishes by some of the clergy had been, and continued to be, a source of resentment and unrest in diverse sections of the population.

Sir John Wray of Glentworth near Lincoln, a prominent knight who was a patron of puritan preachers and a friend of Bishop Williams, had during the 1620s spoken out against idolatry in the church and had demanded a thorough reformation of church procedure. Members of the Wray family were later to become convinced Friends after the visit by George Fox in 1654.

An entry in the Lincoln Quaker records of the death in 1657 of Ann Pigott, of Bailgate, Lincoln, a Friend during those first years, may be valuable evidence that early dissension and radical religious thinking had continued throughout more than one generation within families, for Thomas Pigott of Lincoln, and later of the Isle of Axholme, was a follower of John Smith. John Smith, a Fellow of Christ's College Cambridge, was an Anglican city preacher in Lincoln in 1600. He renounced his Anglican Orders and formed Baptist churches in Lincoln and Gainsborough. His plea for adult and self-baptism influenced many people throughout the county and his influence remained even after he and many of his followers had emigrated to the Netherlands to escape persecution. It was also from Gainsborough and Scrooby that some members of that intrepid group of puritans – the Pilgrim Fathers – had first originated before going to the Netherlands and then, in 1620, making their historic voyage in the ship *Mayflower* to America.

The journeys of George Fox are remarkable when seen against the background of the troubled closing years of the Civil War and the disturbance and distress amongst the population which the execution of Charles I in 1649 must have generated. Throughout that turmoil George Fox was steadily journeying and preaching through counties and towns, many of which had distinct loyalties towards one side or the other of the conflict, whilst, in other areas, there were constantly changing loyalties as the troops of each side gained or lost ground. The city of Lincoln was in the unhappy position of being placed between the warring sides with royalists to the south and west and parliamentarians to the north, and the city suffered much distress throughout the Civil War as battles and skirmishes took place in the county. An entry in the *Calendar of State Papers* for June 1648 records that risings took place in the city against the parliamentary forces whilst in July the city was captured by royalist troops and then, almost immediately, retaken by the parliamentarians. The citizens, no doubt, gained nothing but trouble from the battles. Sir Francis Hill in his *History of Lincoln* writes of the appalling destruction and squalor endured by the citizens in 1648 'because of these military manoeuvres'.

Throughout the Civil War there were constant complaints to the authorities by the sheriffs of Lincoln about troops, from both sides, taking free quarter and of severe pillaging and destruction by the troops. It is not surprising therefore that many people, caught up into the dilemma of being in a divided situation and fearful for their safety, changed their allegiance and their loyalty as the opposing sides gained or lost victories. And it is not surprising that oaths of allegiance became a matter of expediency rather than a truthful affirmation of loyalty or of a belief. However, as the opposite of such religious and political insecurity was a dangerous fanaticism by holders of dogmatic tenets, with all the tyranny which fanaticism brings, many people viewed the taking of oaths with cynicism and religious and political dogma with suspicion. George Fox and the Early Friends held the opinion that a simple statement undertaking to speak the truth was the only proper requirement. Their belief in this was reinforced by their understanding of the words of Jesus: 'Do not swear by Heaven, it is God's throne...just say "Yes" or "No"; anything else you say comes from the Evil One.' (*Matthew* 5.33)

The news of those first journeys and of the preaching of George Fox had, by 1654, reached far out into Lincolnshire and Richard Farnworth, in letters to George Fox and James Nayler, tells of his own visits in 1652 and 1653: 'I found openings...that I might go into Lincolnshire...'

He writes of meetings with the 'baptized ones' especially in the Isle of Axholme. Richard Farnworth's visits were followed by a visit to Lincoln by William Dewsbury. A letter from Dewsbury to Margaret Fell informed her of his release from York prison on 2.4.1654 and of his journey and time spent in Lincoln. However, as the letter was written from the prison at Derby and dated 24 August 1654, his freedom had unhappily been short-lived.

Richard Farnworth and William Dewsbury were just two of those Early Friends, known as the Publishers of Truth, who, convinced by the preaching of George Fox, were themselves soon travelling in the Ministry throughout England. Their message must have reached the hearts of many in Lincolnshire, for when George Fox returned in 1654 groups of Friends throughout the county were meeting in their homes for periods of silent worship and were recognising their meeting as a 'Meeting of Friends of Truth'.

Those Early Friends must have had great determination. The Interregnum, despite the fact that many members of the New Model Army had been dissenters, did not bring in a marked change towards

4

creating the expected religious freedom. Toleration was limited and the severity of the punishment of dissenters continued to depend on the whims and the personal opinions of the magistrates and priests; there was still a State Church with ministers supported by tithes; and political groups, such as the Levellers, seeing that the real spirit of 'The Agreement of the People' drafted in October 1647 was not being fully implemented, were also disillusioned and angry.

The Agreement put forward to the Commonwealth Government had asked for a firm and present peace upon grounds of common right. The short extract below outlines some of the proposals:

...the people do choose themselves a parliament once in two year...that the power in future of all representatives is inferior only to theirs that choose them...that the matters of religion and the ways of God's worship are not at all entrusted by us to any human power...that in all laws made or about to be made every person may be bound alike, and that no tenure, estate, charter, degree, birth, or place do confer any exemption from the ordinary course of legal proceedings whereunto others are subjected.... That as the laws ought to be equal, so they must be good, and not destructive to the safety and well-being of the people....

However, government continued to be maintained by military rule and, apart from the abolition of the Monarchy and of the House of Lords, it seemed to many of the population to be no more democratic than the Royalist government it had superseded.

Friends, along with other sects, were constantly faced with the difficult and contradictory situations through which they were living and Friends offended the authorities for both religious and political reasons. They could be prosecuted for their refusal to swear oaths, for their refusal to pay tithes and for disturbing godly ministers, whilst their statements such as 'Not to rely upon the teaching of priests or wholly upon the Bible...but that the Light within was a sufficient teacher' were regarded by their prosecutors as blasphemous. Their refusal to accede to convention by raising their hats, bowing the knee and using the verbal insincerities common to that age was seen as undermining the social order and flouting the authority of the State. They could also be charged with vagrancy as they travelled around preaching and, on a more serious charge, they could be taken into custody on suspicion of planning insurrection as their religious meetings were suspected as possible excuses for subversion. The following entries in the *Calendar of State Papers* reveal how the authorities of Derby and Mansfield in

1654 had appealed to the Government regarding meetings by Quakers:

> The Authorities are considering the best way to prevent tumultuous meetings of persons on the pretext of Quakers....

and the answer to that appeal was that

> ...such designs (are) prejudicial to the public good. They therefore recommend it to your care to scatter such meetings, and in future to prevent them if possible. If you find any whose notorious disaffection to the present Government, or former adherence to the enemies of Parliament, render them justly suspicious, you shall apprehend and secure them till further order; and for your speedy and effectual execution of the same, you are to use any of the forces under you....

After the Civil War the political position of Friends could not be clearly defined: Friends were often mistakenly judged to be aligned with other sects such as the Ranters and with political groups. The Epworth Riots in the Isle of Axholme in 1651 are an example of one of the local problems which faced Lincolnshire Friends and is one reason why they, and other sects in the area of the county, would have been regarded with suspicion by the authorities.

During the Civil War there had been much support in the Isle of Axholme for the parliamentarian cause. However, the people of the Isle had a long-standing problem of their own which had been continuing since the 1600s. Their disaffection was with the Royalist Government and based upon an antagonism against a policy of land management. The policy was a scheme where wealthy participants were to take over an area of land to drain and enclose it: as part of the area was common land, or already occupied by tenants, there was a possible loss to the people of two thirds of the use of the land and this had led to a series of riots over the years. Sir John Wray, had vigorously opposed the scheme and had supported the protestors.

However, the end of the Civil War and a change of government had not brought an end to the scheme and the grievances of the inhabitants once again had exploded into a riot. As there were many Baptists, Brownists, Manifestarians and Ranters already in the area and now also the group known as Friends of Truth, or Quakers, there is no doubt that many of their interests and their livelihoods were affected by the scheme so they either joined the rioters or gave their support to the riot.

One of the leaders of the riot was George Stovin, a member of a wealthy and prominent family in the Isle of Axholme who was, nevertheless, a Leveller and a dissenter. The Leveller Lieutenant

Colonel John Lillburne, who was later to become a Quaker, hurried, with Leveller John Wildman, to the aid of the rioters whilst the then Sheriffs of Lincoln, William Lamb and William Sutterby, were quickly sent with troops to quell the riot. George Stovin died in Lincoln Castle prison in 1652 during his second term of imprisonment there for his opposition to the Established Church. There is no early record that George Stovin, although a dissenter, became a Quaker before he died. However, his son James was a Quaker and he was followed by several generations who continued to worship as Quakers.

These early years of the Interregnum were to prove to be the testing years for Quakerism.

Chapter 2

IN THE SERVICE OF TRUTH

The year 1654 was a momentous year for Lincolnshire Quakerism and a turning point leading towards an uncertain future for many Lincolnshire Friends for, whatever had been their beliefs and wherever their sympathies had lain in the past, their lives were never to be the same again. It was also the year in which John Whitehead first came to Lincoln and where, when he returned later, he was to spend the rest of his life as member, clerk and respected elder of Lincoln Meeting. John Whitehead, a stocky Yorkshireman from Owstwick and a puritan soldier, was at that time about 38 years of age. He had heard William Dewsbury preach at Scarborough in 1652 and, being convinced by William Dewsbury's message to 'be guided by the Light Within, and by the teachings of Christ', he had immediately begun to travel and to preach in the Ministry.

After establishing meetings in North Yorkshire John Whitehead reached Lincoln in 1654 and upon arriving he had gone into the Cathedral to preach. His words aroused the derision of the people and a description of the incident, recorded by Friends, reveals what happened.

> ...for bearing Testimony in the High Place called the Minster in Lincoln that it is the Light of the Glorious Gospel that shines in man's heart and discovers Sin, he was buffetted and most shamefully ill treated, being often Knocked down by the Rude and Barbarous people, who were encouraged thereunto by Humphrey Walcot who was then in commission to have kept the peace; but brake it by striking of John Whitehead with his own hands, which so encouraged the Rude people that so far as could be seen that had slaine the said John but that God stirred some soldiers to take him by force from amongst them

John Whitehead was sentenced to be kept prisoner in Lincoln Castle where he stayed for four months: the first of many imprisonments he was to suffer. It was also in September 1654 that Elisabeth Hooton, another Early Friend, was a prisoner in Lincoln Castle. There is reliable evidence that Elisabeth Hooton was preaching to groups of Baptists and to separatist groups in and around Nottinghamshire and Lincolnshire in the late 1640s. She seems to have formed a religious belief similar to that of George Fox and her first meeting with him in 1647 and, later in

1648, at Mansfield, confirmed that belief. Elisabeth Hooton's son Oliver writes in his *History* of the visit in 1648 made by George Fox to Mansfield in Nottinghamshire.

The mighty power of the Lord was manifest that startled their former Separate meetings, and some came no more: but most that were convinced of the truth stood, of whom my mother was one and embraced it....

W. C. Braithwaite sugests that it was probably at that meeting in 1648 at Mansfield that, after hearing George Fox preach, groups of Baptists and Seekers joined together and adopted the name 'Children of the Light'.

After Elisabeth Hooton's meeting with George Fox she became the first woman Quaker preacher: she was imprisoned in Derby in 1651 for reproving a priest; in 1652 she was in York Prison for preaching repentance to the people of Rotherham; in September 1654 she was imprisoned in Lincoln Castle for six months for preaching at Beckingham, Lincolnshire and again in 1655 for three months. For the remainder of her life Elisabeth travelled in the Ministry at home and abroad suffering many hardships until her death in Jamaica in 1672.

From the records of Sufferings and of business meetings minutes it is possible to gain some knowledge of the areas where many of those Early Friends were to be found in Lincolnshire. And, from existing records of births, marriages and deaths and from information that can be gained from their Wills it is also possible to estimate the ages and the status of some of those Friends. The records show that their ages ranged through three generations, with all three generations often being represented in one family. Those Friends who lived within the city boundary were, when imprisoned, placed in the city gaol which was in the downhill part of the town at the gateway known as the Stonebow, whilst those Friends from outside of the boundary were imprisoned in Lincoln Castle.

Friends came from all levels of society. Some Friends in the city of Lincoln were landholders and connected with agriculture but many were merchants, doctors and other professional people, and craftsmen. The majority of Friends in the rural areas were landholders, yeomen and graziers and often had property in more than one area. There were husbandmen, cottagers and labourers. However, the term labourer when applied to those Early Friends can be misleading as many of them were the sons of yeomen and, the term of husbandmen can be equally misleading as some of their wills show that their status and property could not be distinguished from that of yeoman Friends. It is not always possible to know the exact location of the houses of Early Friends unless the house or the area is specifically referred to in the Minutes, or in the deeds of Quaker property or the wills of Friends.

Those Friends in the city of Lincoln who visited John and Elisabeth in prison and who were themselves soon to experience persecution and imprisonment were in a particularly difficult position because of their professional or business status in the city. Lincoln was the religious and political centre for the county with a population of approximately 3,500 and, then as now, Lincoln was geographically divided into uphill and downhill areas.

The Cathedral stands uphill – its towers soaring into the sky: it dominates the city and the Trent valley below and it can be seen for many miles across the Lincolnshire countryside. The Castle is nearby and the turrets and the walls of the Castle would have been fearful reminders of the dungeons within those walls. In the area around the Cathedral Close lived the clerics, the lawyers and the merchants, and some influential country families maintained their town houses in the area.

The area was not large and the population was small; therefore, and because of the status of the inhabitants, it was a close society that lived there, and it would certainly have been more politic and more comfortable for any Friends living in that area not to have been in dissent from those in power and from their neighbours.

It is possible to know something about only a few of those first Lincoln Friends. However, we have already met Robert Craven and his wife: 1654 was his year of office as sheriff, a position that demanded that he should not leave the county during that time. It shows the strength of his new-found convincement to the message of George Fox that he risked his position and standing in the city by immediately journeying with George Fox to Derbyshire. During March 1655 he was away again in London with George Fox and it was whilst there that he, with Thomas Aldam, on 5 March 1655, signed as witnesses a letter written by George Fox to Oliver Cromwell. The first sentence of this letter made the important statement that 'I, who am of the world called George Fox, do deny to the carrying or drawing of any carnal sword against any, or against thee Oliver Cromwell, or any man. In the presence of the Lord God I declare it....'

Towards the end of 1655 George Fox again came into Lincolnshire and in his Journal he describes visiting Derbyshire and Leicestershire where he encountered great opposition from Ranters and Baptists, but when he reached Nottinghamshire and Lincolnshire he found that '...here were brave meetings of Friends and Truth honourable.'

It was soon after this visit by George Fox that Robert Craven was again journeying with him in 1656 and Alexander Parker, in a letter to Margaret Fell, describes that journey and tells how George Fox, in company with Amor Stoddart, Robert Craven and himself, travelled to Huntingdon. On the return journey they visited Boston where George Fox and Robert Craven stayed for a time at a Friend's house three miles from Boston and from there they went on to Beckingham. George Fox, describing the same journey in his Journal, also mentions that they visited Crowland and he writes

> ...the sheriff of Lincoln and me came to an inn wherein the townspeople were gathered together being half drunk, a very rude place.... I was moved to exhort them to leave off their drunkenness...and turn to the Light of Christ...and the priest was amongst them...and I bid him see the fruits of his ministry...the priest and his clerk were in a rage and got up the tongs and fire shovel; and had not the Lord's power preserved us, we might have been murdered amongst them.

Robert Craven's house was one of the houses in Lincoln in which Friends met for worship and it was to his house that George Fox was to come on Christmas Day 1667 to organise the Monthly Meetings for the county. Robert Craven was not a young man when he met George Fox in 1654, but the Sheriff who had gone to harass and maybe to arrest George Fox became, for the last sixteen years of his life, a firm and devoted Friend, suffering terms of imprisonment and often travelling far from home in the Service of Truth until his death in 1670.

Another Friend who resided within the boundary of Lincoln was Martin Mason, scrivener, who, as shown by his pamphlets and writings, held strong political views and had been a non-conformist dissenter during the Civil War. He was a staunch supporter of the parliamentarian cause and was concerned after the war, as early as 1651, that many Presbyterians were aiming to restore the Monarchy. He was a prolific writer and his answers to his critics were in the flamboyant style of the age with a flourish of alliterative titles. There is in the City Library at Lincoln an example of his style in a paper entitled *The Proud Pharisee Reproved; or the Lying Orator Laid Open.*

This was an attack on the precepts of the Puritan Edward Reyner, a city of Lincoln lecturer during the Interregnum, who was quickly taken to task by Martin Mason for using such titles to the Mayor and Aldermen as 'right worshipful' which Martin Mason described as Babylonian, hollow, deceitful and unwarrantable. He was also concerned about the social conditions which existed at that time and criticised the content of Reyner's sermons to the people:

> Thou bids them be content with such things as they have, though they have but from hand to mouth; with food and rayment though they have no more. The poor, it seems, must be preached into patience and contentedness...but the priests and the proud ones, who live in pomp and plenty, may purchase lands and possessions without any check.

Martin Mason appears to have been fearless in speaking his mind about issues which he felt should be discusssed and remedied: this not only applied to political and local matters because, as Quaker records reveal and his own writings show, he had very definite ideas of his own which did not always fit in with the way that the organisation of Quaker affairs were developing, and, for which he was quite non-apologetic to Friends. Perhaps it would not be too fanciful to suggest that Martin Mason was a 'man before his time' and that many modern Friends would find that they could heartily agree with his ideas, his principles, and his religious concerns, whilst, perhaps, he would have rejoiced in the broadly based understanding and flexibility of thought which now exists within the Society of Friends of the twentieth century.

The marriage of Anne Lammin and Williams Willows is the first known Quaker marriage in Lincoln and it took place in Martin Mason's house in 1658. Martin Mason died in 1688: sadly, he did not live to see the Toleration Act come into force in 1689 and the building of Lincoln Meeting House.

The Morrice family was one of those families which were represented by three generations within one family during the first years of Quakerism. William and Susanna Morrice were the parents of a large family of adult sons and daughters. William was a well-to-do yeoman in Leasingham who later, in 1676/8, moved into the city of Lincoln into a house rented from the Dean and Chapter of the cathedral. The sons of William and Susanna, with their wives, were also Early Friends and William and Susanna's daughters married into other Quaker families. William and Susanna were generous benefactors to Lincoln Meeting: their home was always available for meetings and they suffered imprisonment and persecution for holding those meetings.

A FAITHFUL
WARNING,
WITH GOOD
ADVICE
FROM
ISRAEL'S GOD,
TO
Englands KING;
AND HIS
COUNCIL;

That they may wisely improve this little Inch of time
which the God of their Life as yet affords unto them,
before the Day of their [approaching] Mise-
ry come upon them.

Which may serve as a Caution to all others in Authority within the Nation.

Sounded through one of the Mourners in *Sion*, known by
the name of *Martin Mason.*

Hear ye, and give ear, be not proud, for the Lord hath spoken.

LONDON, Printed for *Robert Wilson,* at the sign of the *Black*
spread-Eagle and *Wind-Mill* in *Martins l' Grand.*

Frontispiece of pamphlet by Martin Mason. Courtesy of Lincoln Reference Library.

Their son Abraham was a silk mercer and, until the Corporation removed his name from the Rolls, was a Freeman of the City of Lincoln. It was Abraham who bought land for the Friends' Burial Ground on which now stands Lincoln Meeting House.

John Leverton was also a wealthy yeoman and he owned land both in the uphill Newport area and the downhill St Mark's parish. He also owned land at Weston and Normanton in Nottinghamshire. John Leverton was but a young man when George Fox first came into Lincolnshire. He was married to Robert Craven's daughter Ann: Ann died in 1671 and when John died in 1676 it was into the care of Friends that he left the welfare of his young children. The short extract below from his will is an example of the trust which had built up between Friends during those first twenty years of Quakerism.

> I leave the tuition and education of my sons during their minorities to the care and fidelity of my Christian Friends John Whitehead, William Garland of Gainsborough, John Mills, and Abraham Morrice.

John Mills was a physician and a resident within the boundary of the city: he was treasurer for Lincolnshire Monthly Meeting for many years.

The financial assets of Friends varied but the wills of some of the early Lincolnshire Friends reveal that they had enough wealth to prevent them from becoming destitute, despite the constant harassment of being fined and imprisoned, but many others were less fortunate. A long prison sentence, or a succession of heavy fines, especially if followed by a disaster such as a poor harvest or by deaths in the family, could rapidly affect a household. The concern of Friends during those first years concentrated upon caring for those in prison; for those who had fallen upon hard times and for those who were sick and who were widowed. It was not unusual for both parents to die within a short time of each other so the responsibility for the care of the orphaned children fell upon Friends.

By 1655 the persecution of Friends was beginning to increase in Lincolnshire and throughout the country. A Proclamation was issued on the 26 April 1655 which required that an Oath of Abjuration against Papal authority should be sworn by Roman Catholics; the magistrates and priests took advantage to use this against Friends. During the next five years, because of their refusal to swear on oath and for other acts considered by the authorities to merit punishment, at least fifty-one Lincolnshire Friends suffered imprisonment; Thomas Bromby, James Wadeson, Arnold Trueblood and Edmund Woolsey died in prison, whilst in Middle Rasen William Teff and his wife had been stoned and beaten by the villagers. Unfortunately, not all the sufferings of those early years were recorded, as John Whitehead was to write later: '...besides what is spoken of there have been many more in the prison

14

for the Truth's sake in the county...'.

One example of how the extent of this persecution depended upon the will of the persecutor is the sad account of Thomas Bromby of Fillingham, a poor labouring man. His persecutor was the priest of Fillingham, Ralph Hollingsworth. Twice Thomas Bromby was sent to Lincoln Castle Prison for not paying tithes. In 1657 'he suffered much in the spoils of his goods and was turned out of his house because he could not pay tithes'. The gaoler, a woman, affirmed:

...that in all her years at the prison she had never known a man use more spite than the priest did to this poor man. He was altogether unwilling that he should have a little liberty to work to maintain himself saying...he would make him an example...and did petition the Judge to have the gaoler fined for allowing the man to have a little liberty.

Thomas Bromby died in the prison in 1658.

As the years passed entries in the *Calendar of State Papers* show the contradictory and confusing situations in which Quakers and the other dissenting sects found themselves during the Interregnum. In 1657 a Remonstrance sent to the Government by the Quakers explained the difficult position they were in.

We are a suffering people under the cruelty of men in authority who disregard the laws of God, and of the land, they imprison and release us at pleasure, and inflict cruel things on our brethren.

They were persecuted despite that, in 1656, Cromwell had ordered the release of Quakers and had asked for an account of their punishments and that their persecutors should be named. Two examples reveal the conflicting regulations that existed. A letter relating to naval matters in 1657 to the governing Council stated, 'We cannot find that any of the Ship's company of the Lizard are *tainted* with Quakerism.' In comparison to that statement a Committee for Safety and for the Nominations of Officers in the army in 1659 declared: 'Whilst some officers were dismissed as base, debauched, with a lack of piety, Daniel Davies was *retained* as Quartermaster, he being a thorough Quaker.'

In 1655 there had been concern by the inhabitants of the city of Lincoln about the behaviour of a 'corrupt mayor'. The citizens, weary after the disorganisation created by the Civil War, and now fearful of corruption, sent pleas to the Government which expressed their apprehension about 'disorders in the government of the city' and 'irregular proceedings'. Friends living in the city would have taken part in the general concern, but whatever they may have thought about the

Mayor, an opinion was about to be voiced to the Mayor himself in no uncertain terms – Friends were about to be visited by Friend sea captain Robert Fowler of Bridlington.

Robert Fowler had been convinced about the same time as John Whitehead on hearing William Dewsbury preach in Yorkshire and had himself begun to travel and to preach in the ministry. The extract below is from a letter he wrote to George Fox about that journey to Lincoln and it reveals that the captain, who was later to sail the unwieldy ship *The Woodhouse* across the Atlantic taking Friends to America, had no fears of sailing against the winds of political and religious tension. The extract allows him to speak for himself about the incident and it evokes in the reader, perhaps by his use of what was, even for the seventeenth century, very basic English, a sense of urgency and also a sense of Robert's capacity for a headlong involvement into a political and dangerous situation.

> ...on the 4th day I had slep in an alehouse in Stockwith wher was a drunken kru...

Appalled by their behaviour and language and, at the risk to life and limb, Robert did not hesitate to face the rough and unruly band and urge them to 'turn to Christ'. He then continues:

> ...on 5th day kald at John Smeths at ganesbrow [Gainsborough]. Lay on 5th nit at Lincolne in Stephen Fowler's house who is brother to me. the 6th I was strongly moved to goe to the mare and ther to bid him not to ber the sword in name but to strike at drunkness, drunkardes, hormasters, lires.

There is no written evidence that Stephen Fowler, Robert's brother, was a Quaker, although many of those Early Friends do not appear in the records. Nevertheless, if Stephen Fowler was not in sympathy with Friends then this visit by his outspoken brother must have been no quiet family occasion.

It can only be imagined how many debates and heartsearchings by Friends there must have been during those first testing years. Heavy taxes continued to be demanded in order to pay for the expenses of the 1652 war against the Dutch and the 1654 war against Spain. A minor Royalist uprising in 1655 had resulted in an increase of military rule, with England being divided into 11 regions under what was to become the unpopular rule of the Major-Generals. If the year 1655 had been difficult for Lincolnshire Friends, they were to be tried to further limits in 1656 as the persecutions increased and as they heard of the many imprisonments in other parts of the county. Early in the year George Fox had been placed under arrest and then committed to prison in Launceston where he was held for most of the year.

Religious and political ideas were still in a ferment and there was a general belief amongst the dissenting sects that the Second Coming of Christ was imminent. The Fifth Monarchists were a sect that believed that they should attempt to hold the county, by force if necessary, in readiness for the Second Coming and this was an added threat to the stability of the country.

George Fox had already stated his opposition to taking up arms. In 1651, when asked to join the army, he had told the Commonwealth Commissioners that

> ...I knew from whence all wars arose, even from the lust, according to James' doctrine: that I lived in the virtue of that life and power that take away the occasion of all wars...and was come into the covenant of peace which was before wars and strifes were.

Many of the sects, whilst not as militant as the Fifth Monarchists, nevertheless were convinced that their particular form of worship was the sure way to salvation and they regarded other forms of worship as being anti-Christ, and Friends in those early years shared in that belief. Thomas Killam in a letter to Margaret Fell, written 9 June 1656, told her of a visit made by Richard Farnworth and James Nayler on 31 May to a meeting at Justice Wray's house in Glentworth, near Lincoln, where, with a group of Manifestarians, they had taken part in a debate or 'controversy' on that important issue.

This visit had, no doubt, occupied the attention of Lincolnshire Friends during such a troubled year as they welcomed Richard Farnworth and James Nayler back into Lincolnshire. Nevertheless, a further visit in June to Lincoln by James Nayler 'to settle a difference between Friends is perhaps an indication that some Friends were experiencing difficulties and doubts as they struggled to come to terms with their own new situation.'

However, there were indications that, despite the persecutions, setbacks and doubts, the movement was continuing to grow. In November of that year members from Yorkshire, Derby, Nottingham and Lincoln met at Balby, near Doncaster, and from that meeting there came detailed general advice for an acceptable form of church government. It was recommended that there should be a record kept of births, marriages and burials. Advice was given regarding the holding of meetings, the care of widows and orphans and financial relief for prisoners and the poor. There was advice for wives and husbands, children and parents, masters and servants, whilst merchants were urged to be honest and punctual in paying debts and that all Friends should at all times speak the truth, that, 'their yea should be yea and their nay should be nay'.

The letter to Friends was signed by William Dewsbury, Richard Farnworth and others and contained the following postscript:

> Dearly beloved Friends, these things we do not lay upon you as a rule or form to walk by, but that all within the measure of light which is pure and holy may be guided, and so in the light walking and abiding these may be fulfilled in the Spirit – not from the letter, for the letter killeth, but the Spirit giveth life.

> Given forth at a General Meeting of Friends in the Truth at Balby in Yorkshire, in the ninth month 1656, from the Spirit of Truth to the Children of Light in the Light to walk, that all in order may be kept in obedience, that He may be glorified, who is worthy over all, God blessed for ever. Amen.

When the early death of Oliver Cromwell occurred in 1658 the government was in debt and the weak rule of Richard Cromwell added to the ensuing political confusion. There was now a growing movement to restore the Monarchy and again George Fox warned Friends:

> All Friends, everywhere, keep out of plots and bustling and the arm of the flesh.... All Friends everywhere, this I charge you, which is the word of the Lord God unto you all, Live in peace, in Christ, the way of peace, and therein seek the peace of all men, and no man's hurt.... And Friends, take heed of joining with this or the other, or meddling with any, or being busy with other man's matters.

However, Friends continued to be seen as a danger by the authorities. By 1659 Richard Cromwell had been deposed and Parliament and the country was again under the unwelcome rule of the military. The country began to experience poor harvests and economic difficulties and there were widespread fears of upheaval and strife. Now, even more, a restoration of the Monarchy was judged to be necessary to restore stability, but the nation continued to be divided and individuals within the population were still in possession of arms and ammunition. Many Friends had been, and still were, in the army and navy. In Scotland General Monck was negotiating for the return of Charles II and was suspicious of the motives of Quakers, considering them to be in sympathy with the Fifth Monarchists or in opposition to a restoration of the Monarchy: he therefore purged his northern regiments of known Quakers.

On 25 May 1660 Charles II returned to England. He had signed at Breda in Holland on 4 April a Declaration of Intent, and from the following extract it would seem that at last the dissenting sects, if they were not disruptive, would now be allowed to worship in peace. It stated that

> because the passion and uncharitableness of the times have produced several opinions in religion, by which men are engaged in parties and animosities against each other...we do declare a liberty to tender consciences, and that no man shall be disquieted or called in question for differences of opinion in matters of religion, which do not disturb the peace of kingdom.

Throughout the country Friends who were in prison were released. In Lincolnshire, the records show that 21 Friends were released from Lincoln Castle Prison by the King's Proclamation. That is, all except Richard Frotheringham from South Hykeham who, for refusing to pay tithes, was kept in the castle until he died six years later. The Friends imprisoned in the city gaol who were also released at that time were Martin Mason, Robert Craven, John Leverton and his wife Ann and Elisabeth Clarke. It is reported that they

> were prisoners in the city gaol in Lincoln because for conscience's sake in obedience to Christ's command that they could not swear at all. They have been kept close prisoners for four months.

Their freedom was not to last. The oath they had refused to swear had been to an allegiance to the Commonwealth Government and now a new oath of allegiance to the King was required. However, the magistrates, despite the Quakers' assurances that they recognised the authority of Charles II, took advantage of the knowledge that Quakers would not swear an oath and almost immediately 81 Friends from outside of the city and five Friends from the city were taken from their homes or meetings and arrested. John Whitehead recorded that:

> ...the following named were prisoners in the Castle at Lincoln where they suffered much hardship being put so many together in rooms where they could not at some times all lie down at once, and for several days shut up so close, not having any liberty to take the air, not so much liberty as felons and murderers usually had. And at times friends and relations were hindered to visit them and from bringing them victuals and

19

other necessities. And though some came many miles yet were not suffered to come unto them within the castle gates to speak with them and thus it was many times...

Robert Everatt	William Everatt	Edward Freeman
Thomas Wressle Snr.	Thomas Wressle Jnr.	Thomas Drewry
Vincent Barrow *d 1664*	William Barrow	Robert Barrow
Thomas Barrow	John Barrow	Nicholas Hobson
William Spayne	Robert Scott	William Clark
Samual Hobman	George Shorwyn?	Richard Seaton
William Birks	Thomas Birks	George Hallewell
Fortune Gaythorne	William Thomason	Robert Waters
Robert Sharpe	Thomas Summers	Christopher Edwards
John Elvidge	Richard Parnall	Danny Olive
Alexander Cheesman	Edward Fisher	Samuel Davy
Thomas Mason	Charles Tate	John Davy
William Sawyer	John Cleasby	John Pettiger *d 1663*
John Fotherby	Thomas Torksey	John Thompson
Ralph Anthony	John Anthony	William Anthony
William Phillip	Joseph Phillip	Robert Kelsey
William Burgess	Adam Foster	Thomas Graves
John Browne	William Brown	Thomas Manby
Robert Haynes	Abraham Watson	Jonas Gunhouse
John Bates	Robert Bannion	William Bladesmith
Charles Wright	Thomas Hanstead	Edmund Streaton
Brian Rose	William Willows	John Seeles
William Tennant	William Lambert	William Turner
John Scotney	George Reeve	William Dixon
John Willoughby	John Walcot	William Feasant
Mary Killingly	Lydia Carnell	Christopher Codd
Mary Aistrop	William Teff	William Garland

It was the beginning of what were to be several decades of intense persecution and harassment.

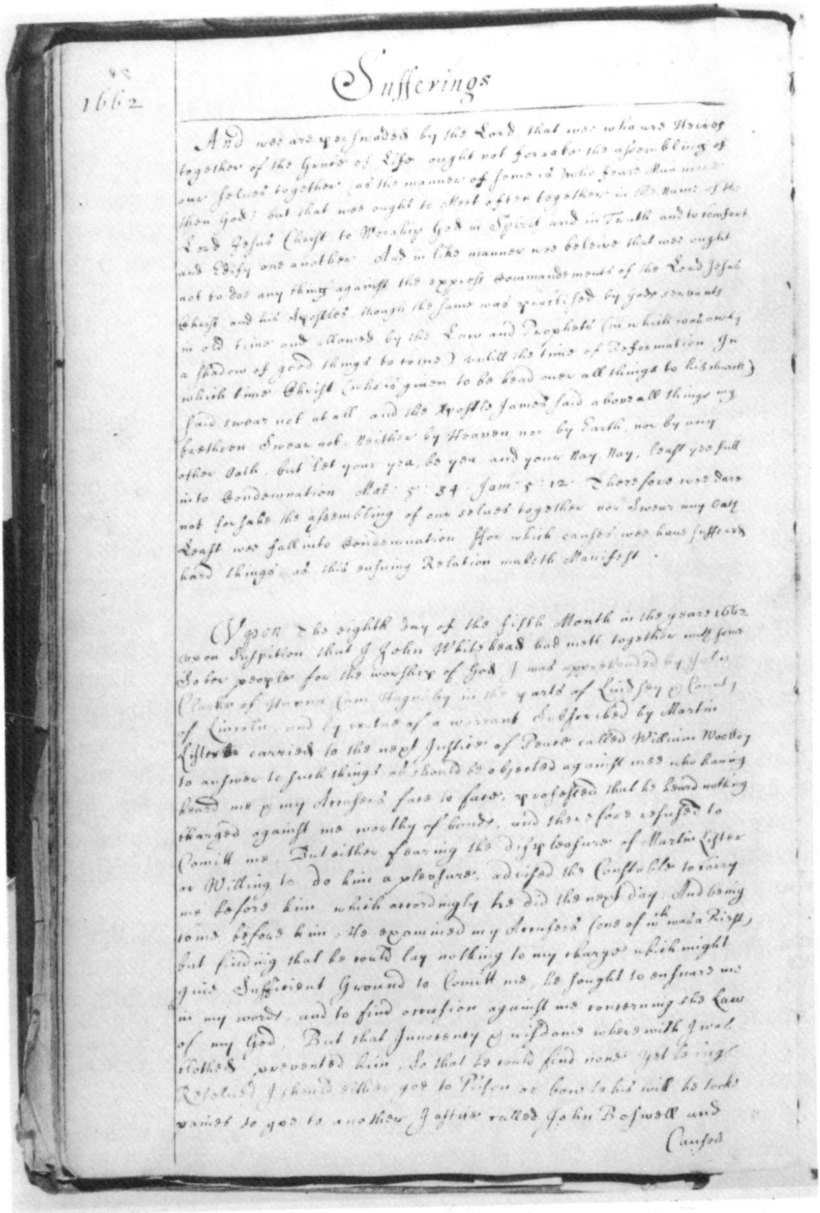
1662

Sufferings

And wee are perswaded by the Lord that wee who are Heires
together of the Grace of Life ought not forsake the assembling of
our selves together (as the manner of some is) who feare the [illegible]
[illegible] God: but that wee ought to Meet often together in the Name of the
Lord Jesus Christ to Worship God in Spirit and in Truth and to comfort
and Edify one another. And in like manner wee beleive that wee ought
not to doe any thing against the expresse Commandements of the Lord Jesus
Christ and his Apostles though the same was practised by gods servants
in old time and allowed by the Law and Prophets (in which was only
a shadow of good things to come) untill the time of Reformation In
which time Christ (who is given to be head over all things to his Church)
said swear not at all and the Apostle James said above all things my
brethren Swear not. Neither by Heaven nor by Earth, nor by any
other Oath, but let your yea, be yea and your Nay Nay, least yee fall
into Condemnation Mat: 5: 34 Jam: 5: 12. Therefore wee dare
not forsake the assembling of our selves together nor Swear any Oath
Least wee fall into Condemnation ffor which causes wee have suffered
hard things as this ensuing Relation maketh Manifest.

Upon the eighth day of the fifth Month in the yeare 1662
upon Suspition that I John Whitehead had mett together with some
Sober people for the worship of God I was apprehended by John
Clarke of [illegible] Cum [illegible] in the parts of Lindsey & County
of Lincoln, and by vertue of a warrant Subscribed by Martin
Lister carried to the next Justice of Peace called William Woolley
to answer to such things as should be objected against mee who having
heard me & my Accusers face to face, professed that he heard nothing
charged against me worthy of bonds, and therefore refused to
Comitt me. But either fearing the displeasure of Martin Lister
or Willing to do him a pleasure, advised the Constable to carry
me before him which accordingly he did the next day. And being
come before him, He examined my Accusers (one of which was a Priest)
but finding that he could lay nothing to my charge which might
give Sufficient Ground to Comitt me, he sought to ensnare me
in my words, and to find occasion against me concerning the Law
of my God. But that Innocency & wisdome wherewith I was
clothed prevented him, So that he could find none. yet being
Resolved I should either goe to Prison or bow to his will he took
paines to goe to another Justice called John Boswell and
Caused

A folio from the Book of Sufferings, 1662. Photo by the Lincolnshire Archives Office, where it has been deposited by its owners, the Lincolnshire Monthly Meeting

Chapter 3

A CHAPTER OF SUFFERINGS

With the dramatic change in 1660 to a Royalist Government, a change not in accordance with the wishes of all of the population and with serious economic problems still to be solved, it was only to be expected that the new Government would have deep-seated fears of organised plots which would lead to disruption and to an undermining of the hoped-for stability. It was also thought by the Government, mistakenly, as time was to prove, that a move towards establishing religious uniformity would contribute towards that stability. This fear of rebellion and unrest, which at times was all too often well founded, was further fuelled by self-seeking informers giving malicious or wrong information and by public gossip about suspected plans and plots for uprisings. An entry in the *Calendar of State Papers* for 27 December 1660 reveals clearly the fear that existed: 'more and more it is daily discovered of the restless malice of the plotting traitors who design to embroil the kingdom in new troubles.'

The Quakers and other dissenting sects continued to remain under suspicion. It was thought that because they attracted large numbers to their meetings they had the capacity to incite a riot or uprising and there were constant complaints, by those who were antagonistic towards the Quakers, that there were 'great meetings of Quakers'. The suspicion persisted despite George Fox's declaration of the peaceable intent of Quakers, and, despite a suggestion that had been proffered on 23 November 1661 by Friends, that six of their number in each county would undertake to keep their meetings free from plots.

On 11 January 1661 (the 11th of the 11th month of the Julian Calendar) an uprising in London of Fifth Monarchy men was quickly overcome and on 13 January the King issued a proclamation which forbade meetings 'under the pretext for worship'.

A declaration 'By The Harmless and Innocent People of God, Called Quakers' was presented to Charles II which stated:

We utterly deny all outward wars and strife and fightings with outward weapons, for any end or under any pretence whatsoever. And this is our testimony to the whole world. The spirit of Christ, by which we are guided, is not changeable, so as once to command from us from a thing as evil and again unto it; and we do certainly know, and testify to the

22

world, that the spirit of Christ, which leads us into all truth, will never move us to fight or war against any man with outward weapons, neither for the kingdom of Christ nor for the kingdoms of this world.

Although Friends were found not to have been implicated in the uprising, nevertheless there was a determined effort by the militia to break up meetings of Quakers and Baptists; many were dragged from their homes or meetings and arrested for attending a religious meeting not authorised by law.

On 11 May a proclamation by the King meant that a great number of the prisoners were liberated but still there was to be no freedom from persecution. The Corporation Act of 1661 and the Act of Uniformity of 1662 contributed to the removal of many Puritan preachers and holders of civic posts and led to the reinstatement of Royalist magistrates and priests. It was now the time for them to seek revenge against those who had deposed them during the Interregnum or against those suspected of being in opposition to the Government.

In 1662 the conditions for the common people remained grave and there was 'a great discontent for the want of bread'. The dissenting sects continued to be seen as a force that could be mobilised into opposition and the Government was warned that 'The Quakers meet more boldly than ever, since no civil power can restrain them they must be governed by the sword.'

There are many references in the *Calendar of State Papers* for those first years of the Restoration that the Quakers had 'the best horses', horses being seen as a valuable asset for any force planning an insurrection.

The existing reasons for arresting Friends continued to be used and new Acts brought out by Lord Chancellor Clarendon added further restrictions. The Quaker Act of 1662 maintained the law against refusing to swear on oath and now made a religious meeting of more than five people illegal unless all belonged to the same household. The Conventicle Act in 1664 went even further by banning all religious meetings other than those of the Established Church and parishioners could be fined for not attending their parish church, and the Five Mile Act of 1665 forbade non-conformists to build chapels within five miles of a corporate town. These Acts drove many dissenters to meet and to worship secretly, but this the Quakers refused to do. They therefore suffered imprisonment and, as soon as they were released from prison, returned to their open and regular meetings. Samuel Pepys, in his diary, has left his own eyewitness account of those unhappy times:

I saw several poor creatures carried by, by the constables, for being at a conventicle. They go like lambs, without any resistance. I would to God they would either conform, or be more wise, and not be catched!

The penalties, which still depended upon the magistrates, ranged from fines, or imprisonments, to transportation. The prisoners could be beaten and they could be sentenced to long terms of imprisonment or for life unless a pardon could be gained for them, whilst often their estates could be forfeited. During the 29 years from 1660 to 1689, 335 Lincolnshire Friends suffered imprisonment for the alleged breaking of civil laws; a further 58 were imprisoned for refusing to pay tithes and 11 Friends died in prison.

Many are the instances recorded in the Lincolnshire book of Sufferings, such as:

Friends were taken from their homes by soldiers without any warrant...

...five were found together in Elisabeth Killingley's house in Lincoln...where they had met together in the peace of God.

...we do now remain prisoners at Lincoln where John Whitehead is one who have no other reason given him why he should remain in prison...

...and for non-payment of tithes are Vincent Frotheringham and Robert Whitman detained by writs given forth and not in the King's name.

Three poor labourers, James Taylor, Thomas Norton and Robert Walker are committed to prison for refusing to give milk, which was needed for their families, in lieu of tithes.

William Morrice, William Bancroft and John Cleasby were fetched out of their homes and then committed to prison because they would not swear...

John Mills is imprisoned in Lincoln Gaol as a seditious person...

In 1664 one of the many prisoners was Martin Mason, committed to Lincoln Gaol for publishing a certificate issued by seamen. The certificate was one which gave the seamen's reasons for refusing to carry out the transportation of Friends against their consent.

In 1665 and 1666 the persecution of Lincolnshire Friends increased with 57 Friends being imprisoned and 21 being fined or distrained during those two years. A sad case was that of Friend Robert Preson M.D., a respected physician of Lincoln. He was taken from his home in September 1665 and sent to prison '...without cause shown...he was required by the Deputy Lieutenant to give bonds for his peaceable demeanour and for his refusing was kept in prison until his death in 1667'.

The goods taken to cover the amount of the fines and of tithes due were often worth much more than the fine or tithe value and many Quaker families were the prey of unscrupulous constables and priests.

The conditions within the gaols took a toll upon the health of the prisoners, and Friends who were free could apply to the authorities for permission to serve part of the long terms of imprisonment imposed upon those whose health was deteriorating. These applications were not often successful and Vincent Barrow, Thomas Torksey, Robert Kelsey and John Greene died after suffering four years of imprisonment.

Friends who had been in the army during the Civil War and Friends who were ironmongers and who dealt with the sale of gunpowder were under suspicion. Friend William Garland qualified on both counts: he found himself constantly liable to arrest and he suffered many imprisonments. The first of these harassments is documented in the *Calendar of State Papers*, 1 November 1662; it also gives some evidence that the policy of persecution was not being successful in containing religious dissension:

> The fanaticks there [Lincoln] increase by over indulgence but are quiet. Capt. Pierrepoint has been sent for to Nottingham and his troops searched the house of Garland, formerly a capt. of the rebels, where they found a peck of bullets and powder and match proportionable.

Many were the letters of appeal sent to the authorities and to the King for the release of those in prison. Visits were made to members of Parliament to ask for their support in obtaining a change in the law. John Whitehead and John Cleasby, themselves in gaol for months at a time, made constant, and often futile, applications to meet with the authorities in order to discuss the legal rights of prisoners.

Friends from the north and centre of the county were imprisoned in Lincoln Castle but Friends from the southern parts of the county were sent into the gaols at Boston and Spalding and, although the conditions in all the gaols were dreadful, Friends in the Boston and Spalding gaols were often subjected to intense cruelties. It seems that the attitudes of the gaolers could affect the severity of the conditions because some of them regarded the situation as a means of extorting exorbitant fees from the prisoners. The Friends in Spalding Gaol throughout those decades of persecution have left vivid accounts of their sufferings at the hands of their gaolers:

...we denyed to give the gaoler any money for our room and then he forced us into a little room, where we can scarce have roome to lye on by another, neither are we suffered to have a fire or candle, though there be a chimney for that use...and the gaoler hath at severall times, and with much cruelty, beaten and abused Friends, neither sparing old age nor youth, and we have not the liberty to go out of doors to ease ourselves. And the jaylor's wife, in an inhumane manner, like a mad woman, came into the room amongst us with a drawne knife, saying "yee dogs I will cut your throates". And a Friend coming to visit us, seeing the hard usage of us, desired that the jaylor would grant us some liberty, whereby our lives might not be endangered, the jaylor answered, if there came in so many as were were forced to lye three on heaps of six on heaps or nine on heapes, we should have no more roome....

The jailor called for a knife to thrust into us and he did sware he would run his iron forks into John Wilkinson's mouth or any that spake one worde....

...and the gaoler would not suffer straw to be brought for us but did beat foul all of us with his cane so that several people passing by said that we could not continue alive in such a manner...

It was not safe for relations and Friends to visit, for it is recorded that the gaolers beat and wounded visitors and often the visitors were themselves thrust into the gaol and kept prisoner. An entry in the Book of Sufferings for 10 May 1663 shows that on one day as many as 18 Friends trying to visit prisoners in Spalding Gaol were thrust into the gaol by soldiers and a constable.

Chapter 4

ORGANISATION, CONSENSUS, AND WELFARE

Despite the attempt to suppress dissent throughout the decade of the 1660s the number of Friends continued to increase and they continued to meet for worship in their houses and in public places.

Throughout the years and as the numbers of Friends increased, George Fox had served several prison sentences of differing lengths. In 1666 he had been, for over a year, imprisoned in Scarborough Castle in cold and damp conditions. He had become gaunt and weak, his joints swollen with rheumatism. In 1666 John Whitehead, himself recently freed from Lincoln Castle, and with Ellis Hookes, clerk to Friends in London, wrote to the King hoping to gain freedom for George Fox: freedom was granted and John Whitehead travelled to Scarborough with the letter of pardon which ordered Fox's release in September 1666.

George Fox immediately started on a journey throughout the country determined to visit Friends. He has written of that time:

> But I was so weak with lying about three years in cruel and hard imprisonments, my joints and my body so stiff and benumbed that I could hardly get on my horse...nor hardly endure fire nor eat warm meat: I had been so long kept from it...

After some time travelling it came to him that '...now Truth was spread and Friends were grown numerous that now I must set up the Monthly Meetings in the Nation.'

He travelled into many counties and reached Lincolnshire in December 1667. He writes in his Journal:

> And from thence we passed into Lincolnshire. And on the day called Christmas Day, at his house who had been formerly the sheriff of Lincoln, we had some men Friends of all the meetings in the county, and all was quiet. And after the meeting was done we passed away from thence to a Friend's house, and I was very weak, and they threatened to come and break up our meeting but the Lord's power chained them, blessed be his name, and our meeting was quiet. And after the meeting I went to visit William Smith who was very sick and weak at that time.

And the constables and bailiffs had seized upon all Will Smith's goods to the very bed he lay upon.

The Minutes of that Meeting not only reveal the decisions made on that day but show the towns and villages where Meetings for Worship were being held. The decisions made were that the county was to be divided into four areas with each area having its own Monthly Business Meeting. They were to be known as Lincoln, Gainsborough, Mumby and Spalding Monthly Meetings. The actual Monthly Business Meeting took place at the house of any Friend who lived within the area and was attended by representatives from the individual or Particular Meetings for Worship. Representatives from each of the four Monthly Meetings met for Quarterly Meetings at Lincoln.

The Business Meetings followed the pattern which had become established at the General Meetings held during the Interregnum to organise support for those in prison and those in need. As those General Meetings had developed so also had a system of organisation where problems of finance and differences of opinion were brought to the meeting in a spirit of worship and with the aim of achieving a consensus of agreement without rancour.

Robert Rockhill of Gainsborough Meeting was Quarterly Meeting clerk for Lincolnshire until his death in 1685. The first entry in the first Quarterly Meeting Minute book reads thus:

> At a Quarterly Meeting held at Lincoln the six and twentieth day of the first month (March) 1668 it was concluded that the Monthly Meeting next before every Quarterly Meeting Friends that are met together may nominate and appoint one at least from every Particular Meeting thereunto belonging to go up to the Quarterly Meeting. A contribution was brought into the meeting amounting to the sum of twelve pounds twelve shillings and fourpence. Which was dispersed at the same time to supply the wants of several Friends in necessity all but the sum of four pounds twelve shillings and seven pence. The said sum was left in the hands of Vincent Frotheringham, John Mills and William Anthony for them to dispose of same for the public Service of Truth as they in discretion see meet.

The Quarterly Business Meetings for Lincolnshire were held at one of the houses of Friends in Lincoln. After 1676/7 they were always held at the house of William and Susanna Morrice. As the Meetings for Worship were held in the houses of Friends, they therefore took place in many towns and villages throughout the county. However, the

Monthly Meeting Minutes do often record the owner of the house where Monthly Meetings were held and these are an indication of the areas where Friends lived. The minutes were not always signed by a

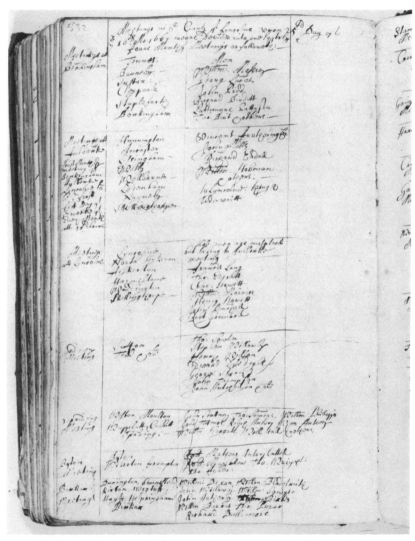

Book of Records: entries recorded on 25th December, 10th month 1667 (Julian Calendar). See pages 38–9 below for transcription. Courtesy of L.A.O.

clerk and of course there would be groups of Friends away in prison at any time when the Meeting was held.

Friends had to travel long distances to their Meetings and to the

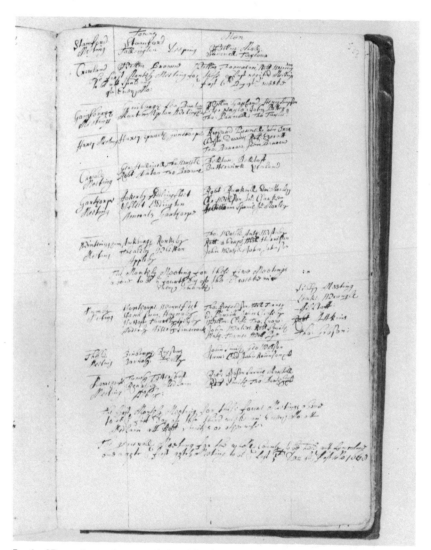

Book of Records: entries recorded on 25th December, 10th month 1667 (Julian Calendar). See pages 38–9 below for transcription. Courtesy of L.A.O.

Quarterly Meeting at Lincoln. They had to negotiate rough and dangerous roads in all weathers either on foot or on horseback. Even now, in these modern times in winter or on cold, wet and misty mornings, it is not difficult to visualise those determined, heavily coated Quakers thrusting their way through the valleys and hills of the wolds or across the wind-blown fens and marshes: cloudy, frozen breath coming from riders and horses.

When reading through the Minutes it is noticeable that Friends, even when very aged, rarely missed a Quarterly or Monthly Meeting when asked to represent their Particular Meeting. It can be seen from the lists below that some Friends moved house more than once over a period of time.

Representatives to Lincoln Monthly Meeting came from the south-west of the county and it is recorded that the Meetings were held at:

Place	At the house of
Lincoln	Abraham Morrice
	William Morrice (after 1676/7)
Bracebridge	Mary Cresswell
Sutton in Beckingham	William Massey
Navenby	Robert Grimball
Fiskerton	John Whitehead
Fiskerton	Vincent Frotheringham
Honington	Vincent Frotheringham
"	Thomas Everatt
Willoughby	Samuel Everatt
Leasingham	William Morrice (up to 1676/7)
Welbourn	William Burt
Brant Broughton (Broughton from 1681)	
	Thomas Robinson
Waddington (Orby Hall)	Richard Stanley
Waddington	John Barlow
Waddington	Thomas Toynby
Fulbeck	Charles Wray
The Manor House, Fulbeck	Christopher and Joan Wray

Representatives to Gainsborough Monthly Meetings came from the north-west of the county and meetings were held at:

Place	At the house of
Gainsborough	Henry Sympson
Garthorpe	John Clarke
Garthorpe	Robert Reeder

Temple Hall Beltoft	Robert Reeder
Cotley Hall	Robert Reeder
Butterwick	Thomas Wressle
Brigg	Thomas Markham
Parke	Elisabeth Barrow
Epworth	Christopher Edwards
Epworth	John Pilsworth
Epworth	Richard Parnell
Haxey	John Pilsworth
Crowle	Robert Scott
Crowle	Thomas Scott
Crowle	William Berrier
Crowle	Robert Ashton
Baland	Robert Ashton

Representatives to Mumby Monthly Meetings came from the north-east of the county and the meetings were held at:

Place	At the house of
Partney Mills	Thomas Browne
Partney Mills	Sarah Browne
Partney Mills	John Burton
Partney Mills	William Pidd
Partney Mills	John Watts
Partney Mills	Thomas Wressle

Representatives to Spalding Monthly Meeting came from the south-east of the county and the meetings were held at:

Place	At the house of
Spalding	William Phillips
Spalding	Thomas Seymour

The shortness of the lists for Mumby and Spalding is not an indication that there were fewer Quakers in those areas, because at that time the largest groups were those farthest away from the city of Lincoln.

The Business Meetings Minutes for Lincolnshire show the Friends' continuing concern for the care of prisoners, the sick and needy and of orphans. In Lincoln Castle a room was rented for the prisoners by Quarterly Meeting at a cost of £6 a year with a weaving loom installed so that prisoners could earn something toward the financial support for their families. The burials of Friends took place on their own land or land owned by other Friends and were conducted as for a Meeting for

Worship, with the ministry being given by Friends. However, there was now a concern that the Meetings should acquire their own communal burial grounds and that registers should be kept of births, marriages and deaths. Therefore, an entry in the Monthly Meeting Book for 18 September 1668 reads thus:

> It is judged expedient and also very necessary that Friends belonging to the several Meetings in this county do their utmost endeavours to procure the settlement of burying places that they may remain certain to posterity; that they may not depend upon the wills of others but settled to Friends of the whole Meeting.

In 1669 Abraham Morrice purchased land in Newland in the city of Lincoln for use as a Quaker burial ground. The names attached to the deeds for the Lincoln burial ground are interesting inasmuch that they give further information about those seventeenth century Quakers – where they lived and of their occupations.

Friends were particularly careful that the interests and financial affairs of the widows and children of Friends were watched over because in many cases the relatives of the deceased husband were not Quakers and therefore did not recognise the validity of a Quaker marriage and the legitimacy of the children. For instance, the troubles of Mary Smith of Mumby Meeting started on 17 March 1669 when her brother-in-law seized all her goods after the death of her husband. There was a consensus of opinion at the next Quarterly Meeting that:

> ...she is to be defended to the regaining of her rights and Vincent Frotheringham, William Anthony, William Cliffe and Thomas Richardson are appointed to manage and assist her in her cause...

All the Monthly Meeting Minutes throughout the county, during those early decades, record a high number of marriages performed in 'the manner of Friends'. At least one or two applications were brought before each of the four Monthly Meetings each month. Many of the applications were made by young people which is an indication that there was a large following of young adults. However, there were also many applications from quite young widowers and widows which also shows that there was a fragile hold upon life in those days.

Friends took care that each applicant was free to marry and that both were in agreement with 'the good order of Truth'. The applications were repeated once more and if all was found to be in order the marriage went ahead, as did the following three applications:

> Att a Monthly Meeting held att Parke in the Ile of Axholme 7th day 7th

month 1670 Michajah Wake and Elisabeth Allen, Thomas Browne and
Hannah Turner, Stephen Parat and Frances Warrener all...declared that
they had a purpose toi be joind together in marryage: They was desired to
wait Freinds answer until next Monthly Meeting...

The following month:

Att a Monthly Meeting att Butterwick the 12th day of the 8th month
1670 Michajah Wake and Thomas Browne and Stephen Parrat came the
second time to know the mind of Freinds concerning there respective
marryages and Freinds did then and there declare there freedom in this
thing.

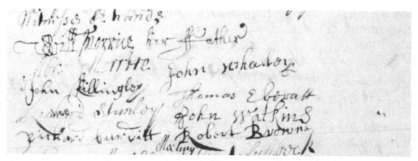

*Extract from the Monthly Meeting Book in which the marriage of Elisabeth Morrice
and Austen Partidge was recorded, showing signatures. Photo by Lincolnshire
Archives Office; M. M. Book, property of Lincolnshire Monthly Meeting.*

The record of the marriage of Elisabeth Morrice, daughter of
William Morrice, to Austen Partridge, yeoman of Gedney, at her
father's house in Leasingham in February 1674, is particularly
interesting because, as it was held on a Monthly Meeting day, the
signatures of some of the witnesses are recorded in the Minutes and this
has proved useful in identifying some of the writers of other unsigned
minutes. However, not all the applications were accepted nor did all the
marriages take place. Friends found that Edward Snaith was 'not clear
from an earlier involvement' when he applied to marry Elisabeth
Frotheringham of Lincoln Meeting and they would not sanction the
marriage. Friends were to be proved right because Edward, within a
few weeks, made another application to marry his former sweetheart.

Anna Everatt of Lincoln Meeting became betrothed to Francis Dent
of Thealby Meeting, a match considered by their parents and their

Meetings to be most suitable. However, Anna became less enthusiastic as time went by and continually made excuses to delay the marriage until an exasperated Francis appealed to Quarterly Meeting for the matter to be settled. Anna asked to be freed from the betrothal and a shocked Quarterly Meeting required from her a written condemnation of her conduct. Anna remained single and had a long and independent life travelling in the Ministry until, in her old age, she spent the last years of her life managing and caring for Lincoln Meeting House.

There were many disownments for 'marrying out' and for being married by a priest, but at a Monthly Meeting held at Robert Grimballs' house in Navenby on 6 July 1671 Joseph Walls, William Massey and Thomas Everatt were asked to speak to Martin Mason and Vincent Frotheringham for 'countenancing a marriage contrary to the order of Truth amongst Friends'. The marriage had been carried out by a priest and had been between Anthony Preston and, as the Minutes record it, 'a woman of the world', a term which simply meant that the bride was not a Quaker. Now, over 300 years later and having gained a reasonably good idea of the characters of those two stalwarts Martin Mason and Vincent Frotheringham we can imagine the dismay of the unfortunate three who were detailed to speak to the aging and rebellious Friends and can be sure that they did not approach their task with any enthusiasm.

At the next Monthly Meeting Martin Mason's answer came back sharp and to the point – that he was 'well satisfied in what he had done and if he had to do it again he would do it'. The minute gives no more detail and the matter is not referred to again. However, on reading through a collection of the writings of Martin Mason, now kept in the archives at Friends House, London, I was able to read Martin Mason's own account of the incident and learned that, contrary to the Minutes, he had had quite a lot to say on that day: his answer had been far too long and far too impassioned for any clerk, no matter how diligent, to have recorded the whole of it. His fear was that Friends would become too inflexible about practices and with not enough concern for the human situation. The following, very short, extract from Martin Mason's explanation would have gained the approval of Friends today:

...but has the practice of marriage been from the mouth of God? An immediate command from God? Some of you mean well...but high contentions rise from small occasions – why will you run into that error?

A widower or a bachelor wishing to acquire a wife and showing signs that he was contemplating marriage with his maidservant quickly came under the watchful eyes of the women of the Meeting. This happened more than once over the years. At a Lincoln Monthly Meeting held at Fulbeck on 5 April 1683 the clerk recorded that:

> Beckingham Meeting report it is feared that John Smith of Barnby is in the way of marriage to his maidservant...also that Daniel Brittain was advised not to have Mary Cooper in his house before marriage but that 'if he needed help in his house the meeting would provide help'.

It is not stated what kind of help was given but it does conjure up a picture of a group of determined Quakeresses with polish and brooms descending upon both Daniel and John in order to keep their houses in good order and their reputations unsullied.

The care of orphans was the concern of each Monthly Meeting and the children were placed in a Friend's home with a sum of money being provided for food, clothing and education: the amount for a period of approximately seven years was usually about £8. The boys were apprenticed to a craft or trade for which they had skills and care was taken that boy and master got on well with each other.

The children generally settled with their guardians, but there were exceptions. At a Quarterly Meeting held on 3 October 1677 Lincoln Meeting was given the responsibility for the three Leake children, John, Sarah and Mary. Mary was a frail infant and she died the following year. John was finally apprenticed to a Gainsborough Friend, Matthew Jackson, a tailor. However, Sarah was a worrying responsibility. She was unruly and difficult to manage. She was placed into at least seven different households as exasperated and weary guardians asked to be relieved of the worry.

Friends gave serious attention to the education of their children and to the children of the Meeting. At a Meeting at Welbourn Friends were informed that Nathaniel Browne

> ...hath a son that is weakley: but much inclynes after larneing he being apte that way: And the boy wanting a good dikshonary and his father being poore John Harvie is ordered to bye one accordingly for the ladd...

The dictionary cost 17 shillings, a considerable sum of money in those days.

The fecklessness and 'disorderly walking' of the same Nathaniel Browne was also discussed at the meeting. 'Disorderly walking' was a term applied to those who, whilst professing to adhere to 'the manner of Friends', succumbed to worldly vices such as heavy drinking, profane speech, or were not diligent and honest in business matters. The Minutes reveal that Friends exercised understanding and patience over a long period of time with spiritual and financial help being given before anyone was finally, and reluctantly, disowned.

As the decade of the 1660s neared its end it had become apparent to the authorities that, despite the persecutions, efforts to suppress dissension had so far failed. Bishop Sheldon was alarmed at the increase in the number of conventicles and urged the King and Parliament to apply even more drastic penalties against those who met to worship in non-licensed places. Lincolnshire Friends, as Friends elsewhere, were not prepared to be suppressed, and at a Quarterly Meeting held on 23 March 1670 it was stated that meetings had been held and also '...testimonies for Truth have been made at steeplehouses, fairs, markets and other public places'.

The second Conventicle Act was passed on 10 May 1670 with the object of making it financially difficult for dissenters to continue to meet. For attending a conventicle a first offence would merit a fine of five shillings and for following offences a fine of ten shillings. For allowing a house to be used for a conventicle the fine was £20 and for preaching at a conventicle the fine could be from £20 to £40. A Justice of the Peace had the right to break into a house, with use of the militia if needed, and to render the building unusable. An official who refused to arrest could be liable to a fine of £5 and a Justice of the Peace who refused to take action could be fined £100.

The severity of the fines can be assessed when it is realised that, as near as can be estimated, during the seventeenth century the annual family income of a well-to-do yeoman was somewhere between £40 to £80 and that of a tradesman £30 to £40.

Of the revenue from the fines, or of goods taken in lieu if there was a refusal to pay the fines, a third was to go the King, a third to the clergy for the poor, and a third to the informer. Informers had always been active during the past years of persecution, but now the prospect of making a lucrative income from that persecution was offered. Friends could still be imprisoned for offences under the previous Acts and it was with these added persecutions that they now faced in 1670 an uncertain future.

Transcription of illustrated pages from the Book of Records

Meetings in the County of Lincolne upon the 25th day of the 10th Month 1667 were divided into one Quarterly and four Monthly Meetings as follows.

	Towns	*Men*
Meeting at	Gautby	William Massey
Beckingham	Sutton	George Lucas
	Claypole	John Pidd
	Stapleford	Richard Burdett
	Beckingham	Latimer Pattison
		Thomas Burt and others.
Meeting at	Honnington	Vincent Frotheringham
Fulbeck	Ancaster	John Mills
First	Leasingham	Richard Yeadall
Monthly	Welby	William Hobman
Meeting at	Welbourn	and others
Beckingham	Leadenham	
	Navenby	to Lincoln
	Skellingthorpe	
MEETING AT	Lincoln	[These men are misplaced
LINCOLN	South Hykeham	but belong to Fulbeck]
	Fiskerton	Francis Long
	Harmston	Thomas Everatt
	Waddington	Charles Howitt
	Skellingthorpe	William Morrice
		Henry Howitt
		John Cargill?
		Robert Grimball
Gedney	Sutton	Thomas Sowton
Meeting		Stephen Wilson
		Henry Wilson
		Edward ?
		George ?
		John Thompson
		John Hutchinson and others
SPALDING	Weston	John Scotney, Thomas Summers
MEETING	Moulton	William Phillips, John Titmoss
	Whaplode, Cowbit	Roger Anthony, William Anthony
	Spalding	William Howgill, William Hall
		and others
Boston	Boston	Robert Malgow, Anthony Cattel
Meeting	Wyberton	Robert Marshlow, Thomas ?
	Frampton	Thomas Foster
Bicker	Donington	William Dixon, William Bladesmith
Meeting	Swinehead, Kirton	John Willowby, William Sawyer
	Wigtoft, Hale	John ?, Timothy Birks
	Helpringham,Bicker	William Barker, Thomas ?
		Richard Bullimore
Stamford	Stamford	William Moll
Meeting	Tallingham	Samuel Taylor
	Deeping	

Crowland   William Browne   William Thomson, Walter Herrington
The first Monthly Meetings for these to be at Spalding the first 6th day of the week
in every month

GAINSBOROUGH MEETING	Gainsborough, Lea Burton, Upton, Willingham	William Garland, Henry Simpson Martin Peter Naylor, John Potter Thomas Parnall, Thomas Taylor
Haxey Meeting	Haxey, Epworth Gunthorpe	Richard Parnall, John Owen? Charles Edwards, Robert Everatt Thomas Barrow, John Barrow
Crowle Meeting	George Halliwell Thomas Wressle Robert Aston Thomas Browne	Belton Beltoft, Butterwick Yealand
Garthorpe Meeting	Fockerby, Adlingfleet Ousefleet, Luddington Amcotts, Garthorpe	Robert Rockhill, William Morley Charles Willson, Jonathan Clarke William?, Jonathan Morley
Wintringham Meeting	Alkborough, Roxby Thealby, Whitton Appleby	Thomas Wressle, Anthony Westoby? Robert Sharpe, William Harrison John Wressle, John Johnson

The Monthly Meetings for these five meetings about to be on the 4th day of the
2nd week in every month

MUMBY Meeting	Hogsthorpe Hagnaby, Huttoft Thurlby, Spilsby Anderby, Atterby Somercotes	Thomas Richardson Leake E Parrish, John Cleasby Meeting William Cliffe, Thoms Crow Wrangle John Watson, Robert Smith Fishtoft Matthew Turner, Wm Pye Robert Attkins Thomas Gibson
? Meeting ? Meeting	Binbrook, Raithby Barnoldby, Tealby Tumby, Tattershal Revesby, Mareham? Ashby	John Smith, George Willson Humphrey Codd, John Robinson Richard Robson, Lawrence Marshall Robert Smith, Thomas Beale

The first Monthly Meeting for these four meetings about to be on the first day of
the third week in every month.

Mareham at Robert Smith's

The General Meeting for the whole County to be held at Lincolne and again the
first Quarterly Meeting to be on the first day of the first month 1668.

Chapter 5

DETERMINATION, DIFFICULTIES AND DIVISIONS

In 1667, when George Fox travelled throughout the country to set up the Quarterly and Monthly Business Meetings, nearly twenty years had passed by since the first years of the coming together of the Early Friends. Marriages had taken place between Quaker families: adult sons were taking the place of those Early Friends who were becoming elderly and a new generation of children were being brought up in what was now regarded as a Quaker way of life. Plainness of dress and speech had become, by the end of the Interregnum, firmly established amongst Quakers. It was understood that they would not pay tithes: that they would not swear an oath and that they did not doff their hats to any, except to pray. Quakers recognised all mankind as equal in the sight of God so they dispensed with titles and used 'thee' and 'thou' to all.

However, whilst the matters of welfare were of extreme importance during the difficult times of the 1660s, nevertheless other matters of Church Government had arisen and these needed to be dealt with, with understanding, if unity was to be preserved amongst Friends.

A difference had arisen amongst Friends about what became known as 'hat honour'. A number of Friends in the country, mainly in the south of England, under the influence of a Friend, John Perrot, were of the opinion that the hat should not be removed even during prayer. John Whitehead was in London as a representative for Lincolnshire Friends and he, being mindful of keeping unity amongst Friends firmly stated that in his opinion 'a man may pray covered or uncovered'. A letter written by Martin Mason whilst in Lincoln Gaol in 1666 gives an indication that the difference had occupied the thoughts of Lincolnshire Friends. The letter is in Martin Mason's usual forthright manner and reveals that he considered that there were more important matters to be concerned about than the wearing of hats: it reveals also his deep desire for unity, and he writes: '...not having engaged myself in that particular contention; being ever desirous of perfect love and harmony in the hearts of God's people...'

It is because Minutes have been kept throughout the last 330 years, and recorded with the Quaker insistence for truth, that much can be learned about the concerns and endeavours, the differences and the unity between Lincolnshire Quakers.

However, Lincolnshire Friends had many problems to worry them. There were eight Friends already imprisoned in Lincoln Castle at the beginning of 1670, and with the passing of the second Conventicle Act they were soon to be joined by others. During the year 1670, 74 Friends were arrested at their Meetings at John Field's house at Beckingham; from William Garland's house at Gainsborough and from John Urry's house in the Isle of Axholme; Spalding Friends were arrested in Ralph Anthony's house and Friends from Mumby Meeting were taken from the house of Thomas Richardson. In July Friends were taken from Thomas Everatt's house at Honington and a crowd of rough youths was encouraged to attack and damage the house. John Whitehead made an appeal to the Justices at Spital about the excessiveness of the fines but to no avail and the persecutions continued.

In 1672 the King proclaimed a Declaration of Indulgence, which brought about an increase in the number of dissenters, causing Bishop Fuller to declare: 'Presbyterians, Anabaptists and Quakers are exceedingly increased insomuch that if there be not a sudden stop to their daring growth I dread the consequences.'

In February 1673 Parliament passed a resolution that penal laws relating to ecclesiastical matters could only be suspended by an Act of Parliament. The Declaration of Indulgence was recalled and the Sufferings below are only two examples of the many persecutions which continued throughout the 1670s. On 24 March 1676 William Bunby of Potterhanworth, for allowing a Meeting to be held, had taken from him, with yokes and traces, four oxen, two horses and one mare. The informers claimed that they had heard an unknown young man speak 'God' or 'Christ' at that Meeting. Abraham Morrice was at the same Meeting and was fined five shillings on his own account for being at the Meeting and ten pounds, in lieu, for the speaker unknown. The next day constables ran into Abraham's shop in Lincoln and took goods far in excess of the fines. He appealed for justice at Sleaford Sessions but his appeal was ignored.

However, sometimes a kind of justice came from others than the law officers. When 11 Friends were arrested at a meeting at Beckingham and fined £86 it is recorded in the Book of Sufferings that:

> ...it is to be observed that divers of the poor people of Beckingham who had monies given them out of the sale of goods taken from Friends as

fines imposed for their peaceable meeting hath returned their parts to the right owners of the goods. Some of them expressing that they would rather live off bread and water than have the money on that account. Others saying they would beg their bread rather. Another said he should not sleep quietly if he kept it judging it more rightly belonged to them from whom the goods were taken. Also, one that was overawed by the priest to be an informer returned ten shillings to a Friend. Thus doth the witness of God arise in people's hearts to testify to the innocency of Friends...

Thomas Robinson, yeoman of Brant Broughton, had been constantly harried by John Chappell, the local priest, and in 1677 the aggrieved Robinson, feeling that the priest did little for the souls of his parishioners, went into the steeplehouse and pronounced the priest a false prophet. He was arrested and the Justices, reluctant to send Thomas to prison, ordered that he be fined, so cattle and goods worth £34 and ten shillings were taken in lieu of the fine. However, the local butchers, when hearing of the manner in which they had been acquired, refused to buy the cattle and the priest, angry that Thomas had not been sent to prison, had Thomas sent to Lincoln Castle for a 'pretended due for tithes'. Thomas Robinson's young wife Mary had died nine days before and Thomas, being concerned for his small children whilst in prison, was allowed by the gaoler on occasions to visit his young family. The priest, when learning of this, paid the Sheriff £10 to remove Thomas to London to be judged for a 'pretended debt' of £67. The verdict of the London Court was that Thomas owed only £13 ten shillings so two fat bullocks, one steer and one heifer which together were worth £15 and 15 shillings were taken to pay the fine and Thomas was set free.

At this time there were 11 Friends in Lincoln Castle sentenced to terms of from three to five years for the non-payment of tithes; four Friends had been sent to the Fleet Prison in London to serve their sentences.

It was during the difficult and critical years of the 1670s that a second difference arose within the Society. It had been of concern within the movement since the 'Hat Honour' difference and it caused a dilemma that could not be easily solved.

Matters of discipline, in the past, had always been decided by a corporate guidance of the Spirit and by a sense of compassion, but there had also been a care that those who professed to be Quakers should not succumb to 'disorderly walking' thought to be brought about by 'worldly matters' and that Friends would continue to uphold the recognised values of Friends. When George Fox organised the Quarterly and Monthly Meetings it was with the object of continuing those values 'and with concern for the poor and other affairs of the Truth'. Those concerns had come to be a form of Church Government. This, to some Friends, meant that with organisation a uniformity would develop contrary to the interests of a movement which had its origins in a desire for a liberty of conscience.

> ...to act according to a leading of the Spirit...to lead from the rule within and not subject to the rule without.

It was that concern, coupled with the harshness of the Conventicle Act, which had brought about the disagreement: a disagreement which became known as the Wilkinson–Story Separation.

John Story and John Wilkinson raised several objections to the now established form of Church Government, advocating that, on some issues, Friends should be free to act as they pleased. Their objections, amongst other matters, referred to marriages out of the Society and to the paying of tithes; 'if Friends became weak in the face of persecution and paid tithes, or, if they met in secret to avoid arrest, they should be supported'. These issues required serious consideration by Friends and one viewpoint was that of William Penn. He contended that:

> ...if the Church was silent it would be overrun with lukewarm hypocrites and loose walkers...or there must be people convinced of the Truth before you could have a fellowship and the fellowship must develop in some degree before you could have a Church....

The Wilkinson–Story Separation is now part of Quaker history, but how did Lincolnshire Friends react at that time? Did they support the arguments of John Wilkinson and John Story? They certainly would have been well acquainted with the suggestions put forward because John Whitehead, always a reconciling influence within the Society, was requested by London Friends to join in the debate about the matter. From the documents available it seems that Lincolnshire Friends were prepared to judge those matters warranting disownment according to each situation and by following the established pattern of being compassionate, but firm when necessary.

His reaction to the 'Hat Honour' argument by Martin Mason in the 1660s and his rebellion in countenancing a marriage officiated by a priest during 1672 may well show that, although he was listening to the arguments, he was averse to being dogmatic about issues and differences and was prepared to make separate judgements based on what was known about each case. From a careful analysis of the Minutes it is difficult to find any real evidence of a serious split at that time between Lincolnshire Friends, or between Friends and Martin Mason.

However, how did Lincolnshire Friends react to the suggestion that they meet in secret and avoid persecution? This question is much easier to answer because the Minute Books and the Book of Sufferings give valuable information that the majority of Friends did not consider avoiding persecution, although John Scrimshaw of Claypole did send a message to a Meeting at Lincoln on 2 December 1673 that '...he kept away from meeting for fear of persecution. However, as soon as he had made his estate over to his son he would again attend.' Friends considered that John's thoughts were more on the preservation of his worldly goods than upholding his beliefs. Beckingham Friends in particular at that time were suffering severe persecution and they were urged to:

> ...bare a faithful testimony in not yielding directly or indirectly to the paying of tithes for which many of our friends and brethren have suffered imprisonment for bearing their testimony against with the loss of their lives.

Friends throughout the country were asked to give all the help they could to Beckingham Friends.

The Minutes show that throughout those difficult times Lincolnshire Friends continued to meet for worship openly in the houses of Friends from where they were frequently informed upon and arrested. Quarterly Meetings continued to be held in Lincoln and at each Monthly Meeting the house where the next Meeting was to be held was decided upon and recorded and, without fail, there the Meeting was duly held.

Nevertheless, whilst not resisting or avoiding persecution, Friends throughout the country were of the opinion that the Government should be made aware that there should be some form of legal redress against the oppressive measures being carried out against dissenters. Lincolnshire Friends responded to the general advice from Yearly Meeting Ministers to send a number from each county to make representations, three times a year, on behalf of Friends to the law courts and to meet members of parliament.

Despite their many troubles the members of the Meetings continued to care for their needy Friends and the costs for welfare continued to rise. There were now many deaths occurring amongst aged Friends.

Robert Craven and his wife, who had given so much support to George Fox, had died in 1670. Lincoln Monthly Meeting continued to supervise the welfare of the prisoners in the Castle as far as the gaolers would allow them, and they supplied coals costing approximately £1 a month for the room at the Castle. A women's Lincoln Monthly Meeting was started in 1675 to look after matters of welfare and below are the lists of the first representatives as they appear in the Minutes.

LINCOLN MEETING	BECKINGHAM MEETING	FULBECK MEETING
Mary Cresswell	Mary Burditt	Joan Wray
Susanna Morrice	Eleanor Garrit	Rebecca Everatt
Elisabeth Morrice	Mary Parker	Mary Grimball
Mary Hill	Elisabeth Pidd	Annie Richardson
Ann Frotheringham	Katherine Massey	Sarah Manton, her
Deborah Barlow	Ann Burditt	husband John is not
Mary Leverton	Elisabeth Roberts	a Friend
	Rachel Smith	Winnifred Cousins
		Annie Oxman
		and any young women
		they care to bring

There were always a number of orphans to be taken care of, and if the month of January 1671 is taken as an example, £2.16s.06d was paid to widows and to those in want; Daniel Brittain was in prison and his wife was given six shillings and tenpence. Nursing care was supplied for the sick and surgeons' fees were paid when necessary. The Meetings bought coal and corn for those in need and rented a house for twelve shillings a year for a Friend who had lost his through fire. Farming stock and tools were purchased to replace those taken from poor Friends by the authorities in lieu of tithes. A coffin for a poor Friend cost eight shillings and a shroud one shilling and sixpence.

In 1675 Lincolnshire Friends managed to send a special contribution to Friends in Northampton and in 1676 to Friends in Nottingham and Leicestershire who were suffering severe persecution under the Conventicle Act. On 24 December 1679 a special effort was made and £24.03s.10d was collected for Abraham Morrice to take to London for the 'relief of suffering Friends beyond the sea' and later in 1680 a further £24 was collected for the 'redemption of Friends who were captive in Turkey'. This plain statement in the Minutes does not show the horrifying situation that the captives were in and the desperate attempts that were being made by Friends to obtain their release.

The Friends had been on ships that had been captured and the passengers and crew had then been sold into slavery. Their sufferings were intense; they were always in danger of being brutally killed and many suffered that fate; they were beaten and starved and many died because of ill-treatment or of fever. Friends collected money to pay the high ransoms demanded but their many attempts to negotiate were continually frustrated. Such an undertaking must have been fraught with difficulties in the seventeenth century for we know how difficult it is now to obtain the release of hostages in this, the twentieth century.

However, the call upon Friends for funds was to become even heavier. At the Monthly Meetings in February and March it was arranged that Joshua Gregg, William Bunby and Henry Carlton were to buy a new loom for the room at the Castle and to repair the old one, and to see that

> ...the room in the Castle is repaired and the walls and floor drained...that Friends who are prisoners there may be preserved from such nauseous vapours and other inconveniences as do infect that room to the endangering of their health.

At the June Meeting it was reported that the room had been repaired and Abraham Morrice was to provide a bedstead for the room. The repairs and the bed, together, cost £9.08s.01d.

One of the prisoners who often spent terms of imprisonment in Lincoln Castle was Richard Hutchinson, yeoman. The Hutchinson family had been dissenters from the early 1600s and for several generations had farmed land out in the remote marshes and fenlands at Gedney, near the Wash. The letter below, written in 1680 to his wife, shows his concern for his family and his farm.

> Dear and loving wife my dear love and remembrance unto thee and all my children and I desire thee to bear my separation from thee patiently and I so do. And I doubt not but the Lord whom I commit myself unto will bring us together again. I desire thee to let the ewes of the marsh that are now lambing be gotten out and put into the six acres and get Thomas Ellis to look to them of the marsh and get John Sims to send some hay for the hogs when they want and put the mare into the six acres.

From thy loving husband
Richard Hutchinson

Lincoln Castle
Feb 4th 1680

However, it also is an indication that Richard's family was not dependent upon financial help from Friends. This was not the situation for many Friends and during the last two decades there had been a heavy drain upon the finances of the Monthly Meetings. At a time when charity mostly depended upon the goodwill of the parish authorities, the welfare provided by Quakers to their own people suffering hardship was apparent to the rest of the community. This was to bring about a distressing period for those Lincolnshire Friends who, willing to believe in the sincerity of those who joined them, were disappointed when that trust was betrayed. An analysis of the Minutes of the 1680s seems to point to such a situation which seems to have developed for two reasons.

The first was that, as the century was drawing to a close, there was emerging in the country a growing tolerance towards religious nonconformity and so, despite the risk of persecution, people were gaining the courage to align with a nonconformist sect. The second reason seems to have been that if one joined with the Quakers, it was assumed that financial help could be obtained.

Letter from Richard Hutchinson, yeoman of Gedney, Lincolnshire, to his wife Ann whilst he was a prisoner in Lincoln Castle for refusing to swear on oath during the time of persecution. Courtesy of Lincs M. M., Society of Friends (Quakers)

At that time there was no formal register of membership of Friends. The demeanour and conversation of the various denominations denoted to the public, and to themselves, the beliefs that they held. Therefore, as the demands for financial help increased Friends had to assess the situation, and from 1680 to 1685 the Minutes show that there was an increase in disownments in Lincolnshire. At Fulbeck Meeting in June 1680 it was said that

> ...some that professed to the Truth spent too much time in inns; in the taking of tobacco and strong drink in the company of people of the world and therefore Friends of this Meeting should be watchful against it in their own particulars and not spend much time in such houses, nor take tobacco publicly which being taken in such houses and company aforesaid scents of a drunken spirit.

Five years later at a meeting in Navenby it was sorrowfully recorded that, despite patience on the part of Friends, a high number of disownments had taken place over the years because of behaviour which had brought reproach and scandal upon Truth. The names of those disowned are not recorded; this was unusual, and could indicate that there had been a number of people who, not being wholly convinced, had nevertheless attached themselves to Friends for other reasons than that of worshipping and behaving in the manner of Friends.

Nevertheless, despite hardships and disappointments, Friends were aware that non-conformity was continuing to gain a place in English life, and it was with hope that they faced the future.

Chapter 6

TOWARDS TOLERATION

The decade of the 1680s proved to be as full of drama and tribulations as the previous decades; nevertheless, in Lincolnshire more Quaker houses were being used for Meetings for Worship.

In 1680 Richard Stanley of Waddington proposed to Friends his desired intention to will to Friends his land and his house, Orby Hall, and to give immediately part of his land for a burial ground. From 1681 his house was used for Meetings.

However, because William and Susanna Morrice were now very aged there was an anxiety that their house would not be available in the future for Lincoln Meeting and Lincolnshire Quarterly Meeting. Abraham Morrice, Thomas Toynby and William Bunby were asked to find a convenient place in Lincoln for Friends in which to meet. This proved difficult because the Five Mile Act and the restrictions imposed by the Conventicle Act were still in operation, and so the problem remained throughout the next few years.

When reading the Minutes it often appears that particular Friends were kept very busy on Quaker affairs and the above names are an example. However, by the 1680s there were many sons and grandsons who bore the same name as parent or grandparent and the Minutes do not always state whether the Friend was a senior or junior member of a family.

Quarterly Meeting asked Thomas Robinson, Thomas Somers and Abraham Morrice, senior, to go as representatives to the 1681 Yearly Meeting in London. This journey, one of many made to London by Thomas Robinson, proved to be a momentous one for him after his recent years of mourning and persecution, for it led to his second marriage, which took place later in the year to Sarah Warne in a room used by Friends for meetings for worship at the Bull and Mouth public house in London. Beckingham Meetings for Worship then began to be held at their house in Brant Broughton.

During 1682 John Whitehead and others were in prison, and Quarterly Meeting was concerned about the high number of persecutions and about the doubtful manner of the proceedings taken against Friends. Thomas Toynby and Abraham Morrice were desired to attend at each County Court so that 'they may be informed by the Clerk of the county, or otherwise, what process is made against any Friends of this county...'. A group of seven Friends was appointed to give advice to suffering Friends about the legal aspects of their cases.

John Whitehead was released before the end of the year and undertook to look after the welfare of John Footit who, for being absent for five months from the steeplehouse, was being kept a close prisoner in Lincoln Castle. John Footitt was eventually released in 1686 and started a small school in Lincoln – from the evidence available, the first school to be managed by a Quaker in the Lincoln area. In February 1682 Friend Vincent Frotheringham was buried at Fulbeck in a small burial ground on land belonging to Christopher and Joan Wray. His life had been given over to the Service of Truth and after the death of his father Richard, who had died in Lincoln Castle in 1666 after six years of imprisonment, he had never faltered in his chosen way, although he too had suffered many persecutions over the years.

In July 1683 William Morrice died, but Friends continued to meet at the house of his widow Susanna. In April 1685, at a Meeting held at her home, she was arrested and fined for 'causing a riot'. Strong words to use about an elderly Quaker lady! Susanna was, at that time, about eighty years of age. Also Joan, elderly widow of Christopher Wray, was, not for the first time, fined £20 for holding a Meeting at the Manor House in Fulbeck.

In 1682 William Penn had purchased land in America, in what is now East Jersey. In 1683 Gertrude Holland from Beckingham Meeting bravely went out there alone. She was followed to East Jersey in 1684 by Thomas Garratt and Robert Pennell of Balderton, Hugh Rednell of Barnby and Henry Pennell of Beckingham, and Richard Parker of Braceby. All were accompanied by wives, children and servants.

The persecutions persisted and John Whitehead felt compelled to point out to the authorities that the growth of agriculture and industry in the country would be weakened if the thrifty and hardworking Quakers and other nonconformist sects were forced, in large numbers, to emigrate. Conditions during the years 1684 and 1685 were particularly hard. It was recorded that:

> ...under consideration of the desolate status and condition of several widows and other suffering Friends belonging to this Monthly Meeting and not knowing how soon others may also be reduced to the same condition it is thought needful that some particular Friends be appointed in each Meeting to visit all such widows and sufferers, not only to give

counsel and advice but also to relieve them if they find occasion...

In October 1864 the Monthly Meeting repaid £5.13s.05d to Thomas Robinson for a journey he had made on their behalf to Winchester to present an Address of Loyalty to Charles II: this did not affect the attitudes of the authorities in Lincolnshire and during those two years, in addition to the heavy fines for the attending of conventicles, there was a high number of imprisonments for the non-payment of tithes. Thomas Robinson himself was a prisoner soon after returning from his journey. Some of the prisoners in Lincoln castle were:

Thomas Wressle	sentenced to	7 years for non-payment of tithes	
William Browne	"	8	"	"
James Dixon	"	7	"	"
John Aisthorpe	"	5	"	"
Edward Chapman	"	2	"	"
Robert Everatt	"	2	"	"
Samuel Everatt	"	2	"	"
William Turner	"	1	"	"
Thomas Robinson	"	1	"	"
John Baldock	"	7	" for not paying steeplehouse taxes	

John Footitt and John Whitehead were already in prison and Mary Waterman, an elderly widow, died in prison in 1687, a prisoner for 3 years for non-payment of tithes. John Whitehead reported that, on his last visit to her before her death, she had remained adamant that she would not pay and had said 'that she was glad she had come hither to die'.

The Friends in Mumby and Spalding Meetings were suffering badly; in addition to fines and imprisonments the constables had torn down the fences and walls around the burial grounds at Mumby and Tumby Woodside. The Minutes of the Monthly Meetings throughout Lincolnshire tell of a continued rise in the persecutions:

Friends from Mumby and Holland are imprisoned for refusing to swear and are in need of relief...More sufferings are envisaged and Friends are desired to contribute 'seeing sufferings doth and is likely to abound'.

Nevertheless, after the death of Charles II in February 1685 there arose a hope that James II, being an averred Roman Catholic and wishing for tolerance towards Catholicism, would also bring about for dissenters a freedom to worship according to conscience. However, the longed-for toleration did not occur immediately; but James did issue a General Pardon in 1686, and from April 1687 dissenters were free to meet in private houses, or meeting-houses, with the proviso that nothing should be preached that would alienate the people from the King.

Abraham Morrice, being long deprived of his status as a Freeman of the city of Lincoln, applied to James II for the ban to be lifted. James wrote to the Corporation requesting that this be done and he also released Abraham from swearing the customary oath which had to be made on admission. Despite the plea the Corporation continued to oppose his reinstatement. However, it seemed now that at last changes were about to take place and in 1687 many dissenters were released. Robert Rockhill, clerk to the Quarterly Meeting who had faithfully recorded the troubles of the past years, had died in 1685 so it was John Whitehead who now reported to the June 1687 Quarterly Meeting the good news that '...a great charge being contracted in Spalding Monthly Meeting by their late sufferings which the King was pleased to put a stop unto'.

An entry in the *Calendar of State Papers* records this intervention by James II on behalf of Spalding Friends in a letter from the Earl of Sunderland to the Earl of Lindsey which reads thus:

> His Majesty, being informed that Mr Henry Burrill, clerk to the peace of the county, and other informers do very vexatiously prosecute the Quakers in that county especially in that part called Holland and being pleased to extend his favour to those of that persuasion would have you direct the Justice of the Peace to give no sort of countenance to Burrill or any other informers against the Quakers...

In that year approximately 30 prison-weary Friends were released from Spalding Prison.

The move towards toleration must have given great satisfaction to the older Friends and for the new generation some hope for the future. However, the reign of James II was to be a short one, haunted by political doubts, by plots against the King and by fears by Protestants that Roman Catholics, through the influence of James II, would again obtain positions of power. The country again faced religious and political upheaval, and in 1688 James II was forced to flee into exile. Mary, the protestant daughter of James, and her husband William of Orange were invited to reign as joint monarchs, and William of Orange landed in England in November 1688.

After the accession of William and Mary the Toleration Act, an Act designed to allow freedom to worship according to conscience, became law in May 1689. In September 1689 Lincoln Monthly Meeting was

given the welcome news that the following houses at been granted
certificates to hold religious meetings:

The house of Henry Pickworth	at Sleaford
The house of Thomas Robinson	at Brant Broughton
Of Christopher Wray junior	at Fulbeck
Of Samuel Everatt's	at West Willoughby
John Taylor's	at Manthorpe
John Miller's	at Post Witham
John Simpson's	at Careby
Thomas Priestley's	at Swinderby
Thomas Head's	at Thurlby

These were quickly followed by the granting of certificates for houses
throughout the County.

It was now possible to acquire a licensed Meeting House in Lincoln
which could be a central and permanent meeting-place for Lincoln
Meeting and the Quarterly Business Meeting. Unfortunately, the
troubles of the past decade had drastically depleted the financial
resources of all the Meetings in the county. Nevertheless, Friends,
putting their trust in the Lord, decided to go ahead and have a Meeting
House built on an unused part of their burial ground in Beaumont Fee.
Friends from the county made an initial contribution of approximately
£28 towards the cost and the building was started in September 1689
and continued throughout the winter months. The Minutes record that
the weather was 'grievous' and only three weeks before the Meeting
House was due to be opened it was written that '...waters and snow so
abound that Friends could not with safety pass...'.

The Meeting House cost approximately £68 to build and was ready
by March (first month) 1690 and, despite the past severe weather,
Friends from all parts of Lincolnshire managed to make their way on
foot and by horseback for the first Quarterly Meeting to be held in the
new Meeting House. As Friends assembled they saw that their Meeting
House was an unpretentious building with a door on the south side of
the building which opened into a room measuring approximately 34.5 ft
in length and 17.5 ft wide. At the end of the room, the eastern end, there
was a raised dais with an oak baluster whilst at the back of the room
there was a fireplace which, at that time of the year, would have been
glowing with a log fire. Long stiff-backed wooden seats would be
facing the dais and hanging from strong hooks in the ceiling there
would have been oil lamps. Stairs led to rooms above the Meeting
House.

Sir Francis Hill in his excellent history, *Tudor and Stuart Lincoln,* has suggested that because Friends feared the Toleration Act would be rescinded, they took the precaution to have a back door installed in order to escape arrest. There are two reasons why such action would not have been contemplated. Firstly, if Friends attended any meeting that was against the law they would have done so openly and would have accepted the consequences, neither fleeing nor offering any resistance. Secondly, the diminutive size of the Meeting House and its position in Beaumont Fee would have meant that escape would have been impossible whether Friends had left by either a front or a back door.

That Friends, remembering their difficulties during the past years, would offer thankful prayers is understood and they also would have had a fervent hope that their new Meeting House would continue to stand firm and welcoming for many years in the future.

That first Meeting was no doubt a joyous one, especially as the marriage of Abraham Morrice, senior, and Isabel Yeamans took place in the Meeting House during that day. Abraham's wife Elisabeth had died two years previously and Isabel had been widowed for some time. Isabel was one of the seven daughters of Margaret and Judge Fell and therefore when the widowed Margaret Fell married George Fox, Isabel became step-daughter to George Fox. George Fox was beloved by all his step-daughters and in 1677, whilst he was travelling in the Ministry throughout Germany and Holland, it had been Isabel who had travelled with him to give him support and help. Isabel and Abraham started their married life in a house in the parish of St Michael in Lincoln which Abraham had purchased from Samuel Everatt.

Lincoln Meeting now held Meetings for Worship on the first day of the week in the Meeting House and a Meeting for Worship on Wednesdays for the convenience of Friends visiting the city. Quarterly and Monthly Meetings were always held in the mornings, often in the summer as early as seven or eight o'clock, with special meetings for Elders as early as six o'clock. The Friends who travelled from afar stayed and stabled their horses at the Reindeer Inn. This inn was probably situated where the Midland Bank now stands, near the Stonebow in the High Street: at other times they stayed at the Packhorse Inn in St Mark's parish.

An Act of Indemnity in 1690 meant that Friends in the Lincoln gaols were released, and for the first time it could be recorded that there were no prisoners, or 'that none had died that year in prison'. Alas, the

A. E. F. WRIGHT

The Old Meeting House, Lincoln, 1689. Drawn by A. E. F. Wright.

indemnity did not protect Friends for long from imprisonment for the non-payment of tithes. The release was also too late for John Killingly who died soon after his release and his widow Ann was pressed to pay the fine that was owing: she refused, and was sent into Lincoln Castle where she was kept until she died in 1693.

Friends in Lincolnshire were once more in prison, and heavy snow again caused hardship. The war in Ireland waged by William III during 1689 to 1692 inflicted great suffering on the Irish population and somehow, despite the heavy expenses being borne by Friends in Lincolnshire, they managed to collect £89.14s.00d. for those Irish Quakers who had lost homes and land during the war.

From 1693 to 1699 England experienced poor harvests and recessions of trade, whilst severe flooding throughout the county of Lincolnshire in 1697 increased the problems. Entries in the Quaker Minutes refer to those 'hard times' and that 'food was dear' and

> ...the poore increases amongst us by theese hard seasons...and there should be noe lacke amongst them and the women of Lincoln Monthly Meeting are to collect for the defraying of the said charges...

In 1693 a strange event caused much pain and bewilderment to Lincolnshire Friends. Even now it seems to have an air of mystery about it. Christopher Wray, son of Christopher and Joan Wray, was accused of stealing twelve sheep. The evidence seems to have been conclusive but, as it is recorded in the Minutes, 'Why would he do such a thing? Why would he who is a wealthy man deprive a poorer man of his sheep?'

The disgraced Christopher Wray went to America, and his mother Joan died soon after, broken-hearted. The Manor House in which so many Meetings for worship had been held throughout all the years of persecution was then no longer available for Friends.

Licences for more Meeting Houses continued to be applied for throughout Lincolnshire, including William Burtt's house at Welbourn, Thomas Pidd's house at Beckingham and George Good's house at Navenby. A new Meeting House was built at Waddington in 1695 on land left to Friends by Richard Stanley and a new Monthly Meeting was commenced at Stamford. Abraham and Isabel Morrice worked unceasingly to obtain pardons for prisoners and by their efforts several Friends were set at liberty. A new gaoler at the prison agreed to continue to allow Friends to pay the usual rent for a room for any of the

The Friends' Meeting House, Lincoln. Built in 1689, sketched 1855, and repaired immediately after. © Lincoln Meeting, Society of Friends (Quakers).

56

Friends who were prisoners.

Toleration, despite the passing of the Toleration Act, proved to be limited and Quarterly Meeting, concerned about the number of Friends suffering persecution, appointed one or two Friends: '...to speak with the men that are chosen Members of Parliament that they may endeavour to redress our grievances...'.

Friends continued to make pleas to their own Members of Parliament for a change in the law concerning the swearing of oaths and to seek permission to make an acceptable form of affirmation instead of being subject to arrest for not swearing on oath. An Affirmation: '*I do declare in the presence of the Almighty God the Witness of the truth of what I say...*' was put forward in 1695 and was thought by the Bishops as being too far removed from an oath and was thought by Quakers to be too much like an oath. Many were the discussions at Lincolnshire Quarterly and Monthly Meetings about this problem, and in 1701 Thomas Robinson, Samuel Everitt, Edward Gillyat and Robert Collyer went on a journey to Parliament which proved unsuccessful and the problem remained unsolved.

Since the death of Robert Rockhill John Whitehead had acted as clerk to Lincoln Monthly Meeting and the Quarterly Meeting but the Minutes for 30 September 1696 were signed by Thomas Robinson and read thus:

> Att oure Munthly Meeteing Held at Lincolne the 30th day of the 7th month 1696 which in its proper Coarse should a beene kept at Wadington the day Following that is to say on the 1st of the 8th mon: at Wadington: but it haveing pleased the Lord to take from amongst us oure deare freind and Elder Brother by death John Whitehead that had been sarvisable in his day and time: whoe was to be Buried the First of the 8th Mon:1696 from his house at Fiskerton and carried to be intered in oure graveyard in Lincolne which was dun accordingly and was acumpanied by many Freinds. This was the reson the mon:meeteing was not held at Wadington as aforesd:

From the time he had arrived in Lincoln in 1654 John Whitehead's life had been truly 'serviceable in its day' to Lincoln Friends and to Lincoln Meeting.

It was in the year after John Whitehead's death that the now accepted Quaker word 'weighty' first begins to appear in the Minutes when referring to long-standing Friends. And, as the seventeenth century neared its end it is noticeable that the tone of the Minutes of both Quarterly and Monthly Meetings begins to change: there are more references to the necessity of upholding Quaker values; of attention to plainness of dress and of speech. An entry of 21 June 1699 reads:

> ...that weighty elder Brethren and Sisters meete together in the morneing on each Quarterly Meeteing day before the other meeteing begins, to wate upon the Lord together...and that the Epistle which was sent down by yearely meeteing in manuscript exhorting all to keepe faithfull in our testimoneys to the Truth be redd.

Thomas Toynby, senior, of Waddington and William Sampson of Lincoln Meeting were appointed overseers:

> ...to see that Freinds belonging to the sd: meeteing doe walke Blamelessly according to the Blessed Truth we profess:...and to continew in this sarviss untill this meeteing shall see good to appoynt others.

> ...coppys of the wholesum orders are sent to each munthly meeteing...and its desired that all overseers and others doe put the same in due pracktise...

The turbulent and often violent seventeenth century was drawing to a close. Back in 1654, in Northampton, a magistrate had denounced John Whitehead as a seditious person, 'one who would turn the world upside down'. For England, the world had turned upside down and dissenters certainly had played a part in the events of the seventeenth century. However, other influences had been moving England towards change. At the start of the century Elizabeth I and James I had believed that they possessed a divine right to rule, but Charles I had been executed after a bloody and divisive civil war, and through the turmoil of that civil war new ideas and political and religious change had been released and had erupted – never to be submerged again.

The Early Friends had lived through rousing, sometimes adventurous, but always dangerous times. When they had sought to withdraw from the world about them in order to spend a time of silent worship they had never known whether the silence would be harshly broken; whether they would return to their own homes unscathed, or have to suffer yet another term of imprisonment. Now, at the end of the century, it was a least possible for their descendants to worship according to their consciences. Lincolnshire Friends were now a new generation which had seen its parents suffer many hardships, but it was a generation that was facing a new century: a century in which moderation was to be sought and religious enthusiasm avoided: it was to be a century in which inventiveness and thrift would create new opportunities for agriculture, industry and trade.

Chapter 7

QUIETISM AND THE AGE OF SCIENCE AND REASON

The years of the reign of Queen Anne 1702–1714 were marred by England being involved in almost continual diplomatic manoeuvres and trade wars between the European States: this resulted in high taxation and one outcome of those wars was that England gained the monopoly for the right to carry out the slave trade to the Spanish American Colonies.

In 1704 the Queen inaugurated Queen Anne's Bounty, from which were paid funds to poor clergymen. This lessened the rancour in the hearts of some priests, although there still remained much hostility from many priests and magistrates towards the dissenting sects. It was also thought by Anglican churchmen that the Toleration Act now made it possible for their own lukewarm churchgoers to avoid going to the parish churches.

Quakerism during the eighteenth century has been termed Quietist, which may well give the impression that the movement began to settle down into an undisturbed, muffled and inhibited blanket of silence. Certainly the eighteenth century Quakers retreated into a uniformity by the retention of plain speech and a plainness of dress which, as the century progressed, marked them out from their neighbours; and this is clearly revealed in the Minutes of the Lincolnshire Meetings. However, the Minutes do not show inactivity. Instead, they show that the eighteenth century was a time for consolidation and a time when Friends began to contribute in a constructive way towards alleviating some of the social ills at home and abroad.

Some sympathy and understanding must be for that generation of Quakers who found themselves responsible for maintaining the integrity of Quakerism in those first 25 years after the implementation of the Toleration Act, for they had to act as a bridge between the Early Friends and the younger generation. They would have felt it was their responsibility to continue to uphold the ideals for which others had suffered, whilst at the same time they would have had a heartfelt feeling that enough suffering had taken place.

There were still penalties to be paid. The fines for the non-payment of tithes were heavy. A total of £240 to £330 each year was paid by Lincolnshire Quakers during the first twenty-five years of the 1700s. There were, at times, one or two prisoners in gaol and it was decided by Monthly Meeting, in 1701, that Abraham Morrice should negotiate with the gaoler to keep the room available for a rent of £4 for as long as it was likely to be needed, even if only occasionally for one prisoner. There are several references to the kindness of that particular gaoler towards those solitary Friends in prison. However, in 1705 Thomas Toynby and Thomas Archer were asked by Monthly Meeting to remove the remaining loom from the prison and place it into Lincoln Meeting House until its use was again required.

The deaths of both Abraham and Isabel Morrice in 1704 were followed by that of Abraham's son, Abraham junior, in 1705, and the removal to West Butterwick by his grandson. This meant that the majority of Lincoln Meeting Friends were then living outside of the boundary of the city and in the villages near and around Lincoln. These Friends were mostly craftsmen such as weavers, tailors and shoemakers, or husbandmen and labourers.

Licences were granted for Meetings for Worship to houses at Brigg, West Butterwick, Winteringham, Thealby and Spalding, and new Meeting Houses were built at Gainsborough and Beltoft in 1705.

The Meeting House at Gainsborough stands in Market Street in the centre of the town. It was built at a cost of £150 and is the oldest nonconformist place of worship in Gainsborough. The Meeting Room is 32 ft long and 21 ft wide. There is a raised dais at the western end and upstairs there is a women's gallery. A visit to the town by George Fox in 1651 had caused a riot, but now the Meeting House and the small burial ground behind it create a haven of peace amidst the noise and bustle by which they are surrounded.

Thomas and Sarah Robinson gave in 1701 'in loving kindness to Friends' a thatched barn in the village of Brant Broughton as a Meeting House for the use of Friends for a thousand years. This Meeting House, with Thomas and Sarah's initials above the doorway, looks much the same today as it did then, although its thatched roof has been replaced with tiles. The plain solid building and its adjoining burial ground in the beautiful village of Brant Broughton now have an air of tranquillity that Thomas and Sarah, because of their own far from peaceful times, would have devoutly wished for for future Friends. The burial ground was given by John Scrimshaw, the son of that same John Scrimshaw who had kept away from Meeting in 1673 because of the 'fear of

Gainsborough Meeting House, licensed 16 April 1705: interior from south-west.
© Gainsborough Meeting, Society of Friends (Quakers).

persecution'.

Of the many original Meeting Houses in Lincolnshire which were licensed during those first few years after the passing of the Toleration Act, only Lincoln, Gainsborough and Brant Broughton Meeting Houses remain much as they were then, and continue to be in use for Quaker Meetings for Worship.

In 1665 when Thomas Robinson left London to settle in that area of small Lincolnshire and Nottinghamshire villages 'on both sides of the Trent', he had found that he was amongst an already established community of dissenters which, in the 1650s, had offered hospitality to George Fox during his journeys and where many had eagerly accepted Fox's message. Some of the names which occur frequently throughout

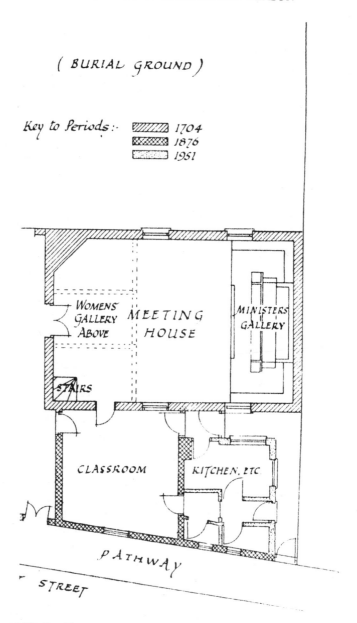

Friends' Meeting House and adjacent burial ground, Gainsborough. © Gainsborough Meeting, Society of Friends (Quakers).

Brant Broughton Meeting House, adapted from a thatched barn given in 1701 to the Friends. Photo by John Gwatkin.

the pages of the Lincolnshire Book of Sufferings and the Minute Books are of those families and their descendants from that area, such as the Masseys, Wadesons and Pidds.

One of the names is Burtt, a family that has been connected with the Lincolnshire Quakers for over 300 years. The first Burtt (at that time with one T) to meet with Friends was Thomas, but his connection was slight. In the early years his house had been used for Meetings for Worship but Thomas was not wholly convinced; indeed, at the first Monthly Business Meeting ever held, which had been at William Massey's house in Sutton in 1668, it was minuted, with regret, that Thomas was continuing to pay tithes and was trying to persuade Friends also to pay tithes. Thomas was disowned by Friends and he returned to the Anglican church which it seemed that he had never left. There is no evidence that Thomas's brother William was ever a Quaker, although he is buried in the Friends' burial ground at Barnby. No doubt he was sympathetic to Friends as many of his neighbours and his in-laws became Quakers, and he was already married to Mary Wadeson before the first visits of George Fox. It was William and Mary's son William who was the first recorded convinced Burtt, and it was William who, in the 1690s, was asked by Friends to buy books and act as Librarian for Monthly Meeting. Lincolnshire Friends had always, from the 1650s, written, published and purchased pamphlets and books; but from the end of the seventeenth century they began in earnest to build up a library collection – some of those books survive to this day.

By 1710 both Thomas and Sarah Robinson and many other elderly Quakers were dead. Throughout the Meetings there began to be a concern that there should be some record made of past times, and John Scrimshire was desired to ask Mary Snoadall and Stephen Carnall to speak of their memories, but alas, 'their memories had grown dim', and Friends learned little from them. However, for the convenience of the Quaker historians of today, most of the Minutes for Lincolnshire were meticulously kept and are still available, although, at times in the past, documents and Minute books have temporarily gone astray.

Such a time was in 1705 when it was discovered that both the Deeds and Licence of Lincoln Meeting House were missing. Messengers were sent post-haste to Long Sutton to the house of William Morrice, brother of Abraham, but to no avail. The deeds were eventually found to be in the keeping of the ageing Thomas Robinson. However, the licence was not found and Thomas Toynby and Samuel Everitt had to go through a worrying time to obtain another, especially as the Recorder for Lincoln seemed reluctant to issue a further licence. Finally, in 1706, certificates were obtained for both Lincoln and the new Meeting House at Waddington and it was decided to keep all important documents in a chest at Thomas Toynby junior's house at Waddington.

The decision was made because of the decline, through death and the moving away, of prominent Quaker families in Lincoln; the support of Quaker families in other parts of the county towards the Society began to be centred around the areas in which they lived, although Lincoln Meeting House continued to be the central meeting place for Quarterly Meetings. There were always resident Friends living in the Meeting House, usually widowed Friends, keeping it prepared for Lincoln Meetings for Worship and for visitors.

The long established Quaker families of Lincolnshire's Monthly Meetings who were able to take advantage of the changing times were becoming prosperous farmers and tradesmen, and their many families had become connected to each other by over fifty years of marrying within the Society. The pedigrees of the eighteenth and nineteenth century Lincolnshire Quaker families are well documented in *The Burtts of Lincolnshire* by Mary Bowen Burtt. The Rector of Beckingham, John Stillingfleet, a constant adversary of Quakerism, wrote in his *Seasonable Advice Concerning Quakerism:*

> They have in these parts within the complex of three or four miles no less than five if not six meeting houses, yet I believe there are not above ten or twelve families or thereabouts belonging to them all.

The families to which John Stillingfleet was referring were large, with relationships extending throughout Lincolnshire. Nevertheless, the Book of Suffering does show that there were many other names of Quakers besides those of the prominent families who, at that time, were also attending the Meeting Houses and were also being fined heavily for not paying church tithes.

By 1711 Thomas Toynby had notified the gaoler at Lincoln Castle that the room was no longer required, although on occasions throughout future years there were Friends imprisoned in the Lincoln gaols. In 1710 it was minuted that there were several Friends' schools in Lincoln County 'kept for the education of our children'. However, in 1714 the church authorities, anxious to keep education under the guidance of the established church, made it difficult to keep a school managed by dissenters, and so it came about that Beckingham Meeting reported to Quarterly Meeting that:

> Joseph Massey, a youth of seventeen at the instigation of John Stillingfleet, priest of Beckingham, was prosecuted for teaching Small Schollars to read and wright without a licence and for refusing to pay the sessions fine is like to be a Prisoner at Faulkingham jale. William Burt and John Massey is desired to attend him next 5th day the 14th of the month.

Quarterly Meetings were the occasions when Lincoln Meeting House became the hub of, and the heart of, Lincolnshire Quakerism. And, what occasions they would have been as men and women Friends rode into Lincoln and greeted friends and relations as they tethered their horses at the nearby inns or around the Meeting House. After the Meetings for Worship and the Business Meetings they would have shared their hospitality, exchanging their latest news of families and friends. Lincoln Meeting House has been the centre for many discussions throughout the 300 years of its existence. The changing circumstances over the centuries which have affected national and local affairs and also the affairs of the Society of Friends, has meant that attitudes have had to be examined and reassessed.

It was still important to reach agreement on the wording for an Affirmation that would be acceptable to the authorities instead of a sworn oath and it was 1722 before a form of Affirmation which began: *'I do solemnly and sincerely and truly declare and affirm...'* became acceptable to both sides, leading eventually to the Affirmation used today and legalised by the Quakers and Moravians Act of 1833 and extended by the Oaths Act 1888.

There were debates on what measures could be taken to oppose the paying of tithes. Nevertheless, despite the Quakers' refusal to pay church tithes it was always understood that Friends should not evade custom duties and any other government taxes for which they were eligible.

There were constant discussions by Friends about the need to retain a plainness of speech and dress and about the education of their children.

The upkeep, repair and alterations to the numerous Meeting Houses required decisions such as the one concerning the desire by women Friends to have a room in Lincoln Meeting House for their own Business Meetings. In 1717 the women got their wish, and at a cost of £70 a women's gallery was built within the garret upstairs, and constructed so that, if the women so wished, they could still join the main meeting.

Mumby, Stamford and Spalding Meetings caused great concern to Friends as those Meetings were financially poor and had many orphans to care for, and this made continual demands upon the finances and resources of the Quarterly Meeting.

Whatever Friends may have discussed amongst themselves, there are no direct political statements entered into the Minutes and there are no references made as to Friends' attitudes to such matters as, for example, the installation of a Hanoverian prince as a ruler of Britain. Instead there is the usual insistence that 'Friends do not deny the King his taxes and not to defraud the customs'.

Quaker Business Meetings are, as far as possible, carried out quietly, in love and unity, but for the first 25 years of the 1700s it was not so quiet in Lincoln Meeting House, for the voice of Henry Pickworth rang to the rafters, on many occasions exasperating and trying the patience of Friends.

References to Henry Pickworth begin to appear in the Minutes in 1700. Henry's father had been an Early Friend and the Pickworth house at Sleaford had been a Meeting House for Meetings for Worship and for Monthly Meetings for many years. Henry Pickworth junior was cantankerous, argumentative and determined to be contrary to any decision that had to be made. Henry's truculence was borne by Friends with a resigned tolerance and Henry took a full share in the affairs of the Society. He was often a representative to Yearly and Business Meetings in London where it seemed that he was just as loquacious and argumentative as he was in Lincoln.

In 1701 there occurred an event which alarmed Friends, for Henry was challenged to a public debate at Sleaford. The challenger was Francis Bugg. Francis Bugg had been a Quaker in East Anglia but had had a disagreement with Friends and had left the Society. From then on he seems to have spent his time and a considerable amount of money in going around the country to argue against, and to discredit, the Quakers. In some way Henry Pickworth had come to his notice and so he arrived in Sleaford.

To be fair to Henry Pickworth the debate was forced upon him, as Francis Bugg was determined to have the confrontation and he continued to stay in Sleaford until Henry agreed to meet him. Francis Bugg hired the hall: he advertised the debate, and it was with consternation that Friends learned that Henry Pickworth was billed as 'The Great Quaker Champion' as he was probably the last person they would have chosen for such a title.

John Stillingfleet, rector of Beckingham, entered into the occasion with some satisfaction and mustered all the support he could for Francis Bugg, and amongst the packed audience there were many of the clergy, the gentry and justices of the peace. Friends could only face the situation with dignity and hope for the best as the expectant population of Sleaford anticipated a night of entertainment.

Friends must have been more than a little surprised when they read the lengthy account of the debate. It had been written by Francis Bugg, published by Francis Bugg and, according to the version by Francis Bugg of the event, Henry had had very little to say for himself. He had been ousted thoroughly by the brilliance of the arguments expounded by Francis Bugg, to which he had had no answers and had made only subdued and hesitant replies. Lincolnshire Friends must have been astonished, for it had never been known by them for Henry Pickworth to have been at a loss for words, and strangely, whilst he remained a member of his Meeting, he was still never at a loss for words.

Henry continued to raise controversies at Business Meetings and by 1711 Friends had grown weary of his then latest enthusiasm. He had been putting forward arguments in favour of a sect known as 'The French Prophets' or the 'Camisards'. The beliefs of this sect were

A
NARRATIVE
OF THE
Conference at *Sleeford* in *Lincolnshire*,
BETWEEN
Francis Bugg and *Henry Pickworth*,
August 25, 1701.
Wherein not only the Contradiction of the
Quakers to the Holy Scriptures, in the great
Fundamentals of Christianity, but their great
Inconsistency one with another, and parti-
cularly, between *Fox, Whitehead, Penn,* &c.
and their highly Renown'd Author *Robert
Barcley,* in his *Apology,* is chiefly Mani-
fested and Detected.

ALSO,
An Account of the Occasion of this Conference;
and how the Quakers Books came to be Burnt at
the Market-Cross; with several Certificates for
Confirmation.

To which are Added,
Two Chapters, shewing how the Quakers assume to themselves, those Divine Attributes due only to God Almighty,
and his Son Jesus Christ.

*As Jannes and Jambres withstood Moses; so do these also resist
the Truth; men of corrupt minds; reprobate concerning the
Faith;* 2 Tim. iii. 8.

Writ and Publish'd by *Francis Bugg.*

London, Printed for the Author, and Sold by *John Tayler* at
the Ship; and *R. Wilkins* at the King's-Head in St. *Paul's*
Church-yard. 1702.

*Title page of Francis Bugg's account of his debate with Henry Pickworth at Sleaford,
25 August 1701. Courtesy of the Reference Library, Free School Lane, Lincoln.*

similar to those of the Fifth Monarchists of 70 years before, and they were prepared to resort to arms in support of their beliefs. Such religious enthusiasm was by then outdated in England, but it was especially shunned by the Quakers for, not only were they against the use of violence, but they had suffered greatly in the past by being wrongly thought to have been associated with the Fifth Monarchists.

Henry Pickworth grew insistent that his voice should be heard, so in March of 1711 a letter was sent by Quarterly Meeting to London asking that he should speak to a General Meeting. However, Friends in London had also grown weary of Henry's argumentative nature and replied thus:

> ...that the Select Meeting of Friends in the Yearly Meeting gave it as their judgement that as he had been a person heretofore as well as now much given to contention they were out of hopes of satisfying him and that he being one that had in effect joined himself to such people who had declared Friends to be apostates, had thereby disjoined himself from Friends so that they did not think that what he had heretofore or might again propose was worth their notice.

Henry Pickworth continued to attend Quaker meetings for the next eighteen years. He refused to leave his Meeting and continued to use it as a platform for his controversial ideas. He finally left the county in 1729, no doubt much to the relief of Lincolnshire Friends.

Despite the dangerous travelling conditions – the poor state of the roads, the danger from marauders and the danger at sea – there were several Lincolnshire women Friends who travelled extensively in the Ministry throughout England and abroad. We have already met Anna Everatt; Anna often lived, as a tenant, at the Lincoln Meeting House when she returned from her journeys, and she continued to do so until her death in 1732. The women always travelled in pairs and two of Anna's companions on occasions were either Sarah Collyer of Gainsborough Meeting or Mary Burtt of Brant Broughton.

Margaret Langdales of Spalding Meeting decided to make her ministry nearer home and preached in the market square at Boston, and for this she was imprisoned in Boston Gaol. Mary Ash, a granddaughter of that Early Friend Vincent Frotheringham, felt that she should make a firm stand for her beliefs and was imprisoned in Lincoln Castle for her refusal to pay a fine for the non-payment of tithes.

It was at this time that the term 'our Society of Friends' begins to appear in the Minutes and for the first thirty years of the 1700s all seemed well in Lincolnshire. There was a new Meeting settled at Leake in 1719 and a new Meeting House built there in 1728. It was reported to Yearly Meeting in 1720:

> ...we have also to observe that there has been of late a fresh visitation amongst our young Friends whereby there appears a great regulation in the conversation of pretty many, and several of them concerned to offer some words in Meetings...

However, there are several references to disownments occurring because of young people marrying out of the Society and of weekday Meetings at Lincoln and Waddington being poorly attended.

By 1740 a change was beginning to take place in the Meetings and it was being reported that:

> ...there is some indifference towards plainness of dress and speech and that despite some new convincements, membership is declining as Friends marry out of the Society or move away.

It was not surprising that Friends were having to find marriage partners outside of the Society, as so many of them were related to each other. Joseph Burtt, one of the sons of William the Librarian, wished to marry his cousin Deborah Barlow of Waddington but at first the marriage was opposed. They did marry and had a long and happy marriage. Joseph became a successful farmer and it is thought that the second T became added to the name about that time.

Joseph's brother William became somewhat of an embarrassment to his brother because of his fondness for ale and spirits. However Joseph, being a determined advocate for temperance, was eager to drink something other than ale and therefore he decided to drink the then expensive beverage, tea. He was, reputedly, the first person to own a teapot in the area. The ageing Samuel, of the third generation of the Everatts, had intended to leave his money to Joseph but left it to John Massey instead, saying 'The Burtts will spend it all in drinking tea'.

Despite Friends being disowned by the Society for marrying out, the impression which is gained from the reading of the history of the Burtt family by Mary Bowen Burtt is that it did not seem to make any difference to their relationship within the Quaker families and that their non-Quaker spouses were welcomed as part of the family.

Nevertheless, there was a request sent by Yearly Meeting to Monthly Meetings that the subject of 'marrying out and of the marrying by priests' be discussed, and that Yearly Meeting should be notified of the conclusions reached. Lincolnshire Friends did not hasten to reach a quick conclusion because it was 1744 before they returned their answer. The general opinion was thus:

Dear Friends,
Pursuant to your Minute of 1741 relating to marriages by the priest...the consideration of Friends in the several counties we have deliberately weighed and considered the said Minute and it is the general sense of Friends in this county therein recommended and advised that we don't at present see any alteration to be made will be an amendment to it, and indeed we think it rightly observed and practiced will do very well, and redress many grievances complained of; with true love we conclude your Friends.

Signed on behalf of our Quarterly Meeting
held at Lincoln the 22nd of the 1st Mo:1743/4
by Robert Massey

The decline of numbers of Friends therefore continued through disownment for marrying out. This was also the time when John Wesley, raised in that stronghold of Quakerism, the Isle of Axholme, was about to claim many converts throughout England for Methodism. Nevertheless, there were still many Quakers in Lincolnshire and those of our Lincolnshire Quakers who were firmly established as such, were now accepted and respected by their neighbours and by many of the priests. Quakers were still liable to be fined and even arrested and were to be so for many decades yet to come. There was still an adamant determination by some Friends not to pay tithes and polite messages were sent to the priests, such as: 'Friends are not willing to answer to your demands therefore proceed your own way to obtain them...'. Which meant of course that their goods were distrained or that they were fined; for refusing to pay the fines Hannah Risdale and Richard Allitson were both kept in gaol for several months despite repeated appeals for their release by Friends.

So, as 1752 was reached and the Julian Calendar was changed to the Gregorian Calendar and January became the first month of the year, our Friends in Lincolnshire were, it seems now in hindsight, to have been at a turning point in the history of Quakerism in Lincolnshire. The Friends were on the whole prospering: they were able to contribute to, and to take advantage of, the economic changes which were occurring but they were still liable to be imprisoned or fined. There was a division within the Meetings as some broke away from the disciplines whilst others desired to maintain the traditions.

Lincolnshire Friends must have looked back upon the past eventful

100 years which had gone by since George Fox had journeyed and preached 'on both sides of the Trent' and wondered what the next 100 years would bring to England, and to Quakerism in Lincolnshire.

Left: John (2) Maw, a grocer and mustard manufacturer, great grandfather to Sophia Thompson. Settled in Gainsborough 1771. Right: Margaret Maw née Harvey, great grandmother to Sophia Thompson. Settled in Gainsborough 1771. Photographs taken from original paintings. © Gainsborough Meeting. (See below, p. 76)

Chapter 8

FROM QUIETISM TO EVANGELISM

The first 100 years of Quakerism had started in the midst of civil strife. In 1746, at the beginning of what was to be the second 100 years, there were again fears of rebellion throughout the country as efforts were made by Charles Edward Stuart to regain the throne for the Stuarts. However, the earlier decision made by George Fox and the Early Friends not to become embroiled in any future violence had by then become a firm part of the Quaker way of life and the Lincolnshire Monthly Meeting Minutes reveal that Friends determinedly kept apart from the civil unrest.

Nevertheless, as political and economic change began to take place and as the expansion of trade at home and abroad in coal, iron, textiles and shipping began to quicken, the demands made by these changes required improvements in roads and waterways in order to get goods and livestock to the towns and ports: it was also necessary to improve the drainage and irrigation of the farming areas. Therefore, despite their retirement from the mannerisms of the fashionable world, and despite the fact that full civic rights continued to be denied to dissenters, it had become necessary for Friends in Lincolnshire to be, along with their fellow citizens, very active in local and business affairs.

As the wealth of the middling classes throughout the county had increased, so had their desire to gain more political power, and the reign of George III was ushered in, in 1760, to rumblings of a need for change in the political system. More newspapers became available bringing information and ideas to a wider readership and alerting the people to events and changing conditions abroad, and the second half of the eighteenth century was the time when there were strong fears that the trends towards revolutionary forces in Europe would affect England, whilst the radical ideas of freedom of liberty and of speech, such as those put forward by John Wilkes and then later by Thomas Paine, were regarded with suspicion by the authorities. Friends and other dissenters again found themselves being suspected of having some connection with ideas of subversion. A dissenter, Thomas Smith, a yeoman of Waddington, wrote: 'I am one of those charged with the disaffection to Government and I am branded with the infamous names of republicans and Painites.'

The expansion of trade also meant that there was constant pressure upon the Government to protect the trading interests of Britain, and by some sections of the people to do so by the waging of war against countries in competition with Britain. This raised for Friends the serious issue of how they could deal with their obligations under the Militia Act of 1762 and still continue to uphold their Peace Testimony. Within the Act, it was allowed that those citizens who were eligible for duty with the Militia could be free to pay another person to serve in their stead.

It was especially difficult for those Friends living in a close-knit rural community to withstand the pressure to support the Militia, and if they refused it was also against their principles to pay others to take their place. The alternative for them, therefore, was a term in prison. For some Friends the pressures were too great and it was with regret that Robert Massey, clerk to the Quarterly Meeting in 1762 recorded that 'some subscribe to be exempt from serving in the Militia'.

At this time there was much anxiety by English Friends for the safety of American Friends, for they too were facing similar problems and persecution. From 1756 to 1763 the American colonists were involved in wars with the American Indians and with the French, whilst in 1774 the reluctance to pay taxes by the colonists to the Government of George III led to the American War of Independence.

As the century progressed there were the usual problems associated with ageing buildings, and all the Meeting Houses were requiring maintenance and repairs. The bills for the repairs show how the cost of living was rising, for instance the repair of a window in 1754 had been one shilling, whereas for a similar repair 40 years later, the cost was three times that amount.

Lincoln Meeting House was the responsibility of the Quarterly Meeting and there were, over the years, complaints about the lack of ventilation in the Meeting house, a problem which seemed to affect other Meeting Houses, for successive clerks recorded complaints about drowsiness amongst Friends during Meetings. It is with sympathy that a reader of those Minutes could feel for those past Friends, for they would have been up since dawn: many Friends would have been working intensively on their farms before they left for Meeting; they worked in all weathers and then walked or rode long distances to their Meetings – Meetings which often lasted for up to two hours. It is not surprising therefore, if the room was warm and the ventilation poor, that some Friends eventually succumbed to drowsiness.

Nevertheless, it is owing to the persistence of those Friends and their commitment to Quakerism during this second century from 1750 to 1850 that Quaker Meetings have continued to be held without a break in Lincolnshire. Also, it was those Friends who gave their support to the many Quaker humanitarian reform groups which became established during that time.

However, as early as the 1750s, Lincolnshire Friends were having to come to terms with the fact that there was, in the mainly agricultural county of Lincolnshire, a slow but steady decline in attendance at some of the Meeting Houses. And it is by the closing down of Meetings, or by the building of new Meeting Houses, that the strength of Quaker conviction in Lincolnshire during the eighteenth century can be traced: where it either remained, flourished, or disappeared in different parts of the county.

Stamford Monthly Meeting, always a small Meeting, had been absorbed into Spalding Monthly Meeting as early as 1715 and, because many familes belonging to the once large Mumby Meeting had never fully recovered financially from the heavy persecutions of the last century, Mumby was by 1768 much reduced, and was absorbed into Wainfleet Monthly Meeting, with the Monthly Meeting usually being held at Partney Mills. Nevertheless, it was found necessary to build a new Meeting House at Wainfleet in 1775 for the use of Wainfleet Friends.

By 1768 there were few Friends living within the city of Lincoln and it was decided to transfer Lincoln Monthly Meeting to where most of its members lived, which was in and around the villages near to Lincoln and in Brant Broughton, and to call it the Broughton Monthly Meeting. Lincoln Meeting House was still used for Quarterly Business and other special Meetings, and Friend Eliza Fowler was left in residence in order to keep it clean and aired, for which she was paid two shillings and sixpence a quarter.

Although Friends had now been in Lincolnshire for over 100 years, it is interesting that, despite the movement away by some of the younger generation, the occupations of Friends were much the same as they had been when George Fox had first visited the area. In the towns, or near to the towns, there were weavers, tailors, millers, ironmongers and other craftsmen and traders, and their businesses were expanding, but it was still the farmers with their families spread wide across Lincolnshire who remained as the prominent families and, as agriculture became more specialised, so the Quaker farmers, open to new ideas, prospered.

The list below of the trustees appointed in 1765 to care for the maintenance of Lincoln Meeting House is an indication of the prominence of those Friends conected with agriculture.

Robert Massey, senior	Carlton le Moorland	grazier
Jospeh Smith	Waddington	husbandman
John Jalland, junior	Stapleford	yeoman
Joseph Chantry	Greetwell	yeoman
Joseph Burtt, junior	Welbourn	yeoman
Thomas Burtt	Welbourn	yeoman
John Hutchinson	Norton Disney	yeoman

It can be argued that what was happening at this time in the Society of Friends was reflecting a pattern similar to a pattern then occurring throughout England. During the eighteenth century, a century when rationalism had progressed and there was an increase in the study of science, there had been a falling off of attendance at all places of worship, except for perhaps the movement towards Methodism.

The advance of technology and industry was creating opportunities for the migration of families into the new emerging industries and the records show that some daughters of Lincolnshire Quaker families married into Quaker families in the industrial areas. However, the Society of Friends had the added problem that there were now even more marriages outside of the Society.

Although the daughter or son was disowned from the Society for 'marrying out', the regard for them and their position in the family was usually secure, with the new marriage partner being accepted as a member of the family with the two denominations existing amicably side by side within the family.

One such marriage was the romantic runaway marriage to Gretna Green in 1797 of Deborah Maw of Gainsborough Meeting to William Bourn, an Anglican, and a ropemaker in Gainsborough. Deborah was the daughter of John Maw, a successful farmer, grocer and a manufacturer of mustard. Both families, shaken by the impetuous behaviour of the young couple, were relieved when they finally returned home to take their vows at a marriage ceremony in Gainsborough Parish Church. The happiness of the young couple was short-lived because Deborah died the following year at the birth of their son Joseph. The baby, at the wish of his Quaker grandfather, was accepted into membership of the Society as well as into the Anglican

Church. William Bourn seems to have kept his contact with the Quakers and he later married another Quakeress, Elisabeth Day.

By 1796, 128 years after the setting up of the Monthly Meetings by George Fox, the Monthly Meetings had been reduced to three – Gainsborough, Broughton and Spalding with Wainfleet. There was concern that the difficulties of travel would isolate those families living in the remoter parts of the country so overseers were appointed to visit them regularly and to care for their spiritual and physical needs.

There were still orphans to care for, and the welfare of the children of the Meetings to be considered. Yearly Meeting had established a Quaker boarding school in 1779 at Ackworth in Yorkshire on a site purchased from the authorities of the Foundling Hospital. Elisabeth Pearson of Wainfleet Meeting, for a fee of £8 a year, was the first pupil from Lincolnshire to attend Ackworth School.

Lincoln Meeting House, despite the fact that there was no Lincoln Meeting, appears to have been frequently in use and for often exciting occasions; many visitors from America and other countries came to the Meeting House bringing up-to-date news and messages. There were also the reports given by Lincolnshire travelling ministers about their own journeys, such as those of William Reckitt from Wainfleet Meeting. William travelled extensively and often in dangerous circumstances throughout Europe, America and Barbados. At one time he was mistakenly held as a prisoner of war in France. Hannah Pine and Deborah Skinner of Spalding Meeting were, during those years, travelling ministers, and when Hannah Pine died in 1784 she had been a travelling minister for 45 years.

Deborah Darby of the Quaker family in Coalbrookdale in Shropshire made more than one visit to the Meeting House, bringing books for the children of the Lincolnshire Meetings and no doubt telling them about the great roaring furnaces at the Darby Ironworks and of the many products manufactured there, which were so important to the new industries then emerging in Britain.

Visiting ministers often gave, according to the Minutes, powerful and thought-provoking ministry. Friends such as Edward Gurney, William Rowntree, Peter Bedford and William Tuke came to speak about their humanitarian concerns and their hopes to create better social conditions for the poor, for despite it being a time of prosperity there were many people, in both towns and rural areas, living in wretched conditions, conditions which have been portrayed so dramatically in the paintings by William Hogarth.

Part of a letter from William Reckitt of Wainfleet written while on a journey in America. Courtesy of Lincolnshire Monthly Meeting, Society of Friends (Quakers).

William Tuke again visited Lincoln Meeting House in 1805 and Friends, with sympathy and understanding, heard of the work being done at The Retreat in York, the hospital which he had founded in 1796 for the care of the mentally ill. He had founded the hospital in order to care for patients without the cruel forms of restriction to which, at that time, the mentally ill were often subjected. Later, in 1814, Friends must also have listened with equal sympathy to Elizabeth Fry who, just before her first visit to Lincoln Meeting House, had been introduced by Peter Bedford to the need for prison reform and had recently witnessed the horrors which then existed within the walls of Newgate Prison in London. The Minutes do not record her ministry, but it can be imagined how her appeals for help and support would have touched the hearts of Friends. Elizabeth Fry came again in 1824 and by that time her efforts for the reform of prison conditions had become well known.

There was throughout those years great disquiet within the Society about the slave trade and it can be seen from the extract below that as early as 1727 an Advice from Yearly Meeting had been sent to all Meetings. It also shows how in those times slavery was accepted even by some Friends. However, it was not acceptable to the Society as a whole and the Advice reads thus:

1727

It is the sense of this Meeting that the importing of negroes from their native country and their relations by Friends is not a commendable nor allowed practice, and that practice is censured by this Meeting.

By 1761 the concern had become more urgent and the Advice was:

This Meeting taking into consideration the former advice of this Meeting, particularly in 1727 and 1758, against dealing in negroes, and having reason to apprehend that diverse under our name are concerned in this unchristian traffic, do recommend it earnestly to the care of Friends everywhere to discourage as much as is in them lies to a practice so repugnant to our Christian profession, and to deal with all such as shall persevere in a conduct so reproachful to the Society, and to disown them if they desist not therefrom.

The aim to abolish the Slave Trade and the practice of keeping slaves was to be of concern to many Friends throughout the 1700s and early 1800s, and by 1774 the keeping of slaves by Friends in America was deemed by American Friends to be grounds for disownment. British Friends formed a 'Slave Trade Committee' in 1783 and working with other societies finally became absorbed, in 1796, into a national movement against slavery. The Minutes of Lincolnshire Meetings show that Lincolnshire Friends approved of and supported this concern despite its being a very controversial issue, for the trading of and the labour of slaves in the British colonies was regarded as an acceptable and added asset towards the economy during a rising tide of prosperity.

In 1788, despite the difficulties, Lincolnshire Friends felt that they should bring to public attention in the county the need to work towards governmental reform to bring to an end such inhuman practices as keeping and buying and selling fellow humans into slavery.

It proved to be difficult to arrange a public meeting, not because of opposition by the Lincoln authorities – indeed, some members of Lincoln Corporation had earlier petitioned against slavery – but because fears that revolutionary events in Europe were influencing political thinking in England caused the Government to view the congregations of large numbers of people with suspicion. The Mayor of Lincoln, therefore, cautioned the citizens against attending any public meeting. It was not until 1807 that the slave trade was abolished within the British Empire and 1833 before the practice of keeping slaves was abolished in the British colonies.

However, as much as Lincolnshire Friends were concerned for the plight of slaves, they were, nevertheless, also deeply concerned for the plight of the labouring poor in their own county. During 1771 there were severe floods throughout the county. In an area west of Lincoln there were 20,000 acres under water. There were then periods of bad weather throughout England with low harvest yields: bread was dear and wages for labourers were as low as one shilling and sixpence a day (7.5 new pence) whilst sixpence (2.5 new pence) was the price of a 4lb loaf. Acording to Mitchell and Deane, the price fluctuated during the next two decades during famine years, but in the famine year of 1792 the price began to rise even more sharply, and from 1800 to 1814 during the Napoleonic Wars, at times of famine, a 4lb loaf was costing approximately between one shilling and one shilling and sixpence (5 to 8 new pence).

There continued to be years of hardship after the end of the wars, and on 21 December 1815 the Lincolnshire Monthly Meetings agreed to:

> ...unite their contributions into one common stock for the maintenance of the poor–some Meetings having a heavier commitment towards the poor...and that all disposable property belonging to the Monthly and other Meetings to be part of the common stock....

Friends not only cared for their own poor but tried to alleviate the distressful conditions within the communtiy. During a cholera epidemic in Gainsborough during the 1800s the women Friends of Gainsborough were, throughout the epidemic, kept busy making and distributing to the sick a medicinal gruel of flour, arrowroot and cinnamon.

For Friends the Napoleonic Wars meant that they again faced the risk of imprisonment for their pacifist principles, although the sentence of only fourteen days in Lincoln Castle passed on William Nainby for refusing to join the Militia seems to indicate that some magistrates were prepared to be lenient.

During the difficult years of the wars Lincolnshire Friends organised a series of open meetings to bring the subject of peace and of Quaker concerns before the public. The meetings were held in Stamford, Grantham, Leadenham, Spital and Redbourne and in Newark.

It was during those difficult times, in 1805, that Spalding Friends made the decision to build a new Meeting House. In 1698 the Spalding Early Friends had bought two cottages and land for £44 and for a further £86 had converted the cottages into a Meeting House. This Meeting House had served them well for over 100 years but now the Friends decided to demolish it and, with materials from the old Meeting House and with £50 from the sale of Boston Meeting House towards the cost, a new Meeting House was built in the Georgian style, on Westlode Street, Spalding. The Meeting House, elegant in proportions stands in a pleasant garden, next to the Quaker burial ground. Many of the names on the gravestones are of the descendants of those early families who welcomed George Fox into the fen country in the seventeenth century – such as the Hutchinsons, the Masseys, the Petchells and the Nainbys.

The new Spalding Meeting House may well have been a cause for satisfaction, but Friends were having to come to terms with the problem of declining membership, for, added to the loss to the membership through death and through the marrying-out by members of the Society, there was also the fact that very few new members were coming into the Meetings. This decline was to continue as the nineteenth century progressed, although there had arisen throughout the country and mainly through Methodism, a reaction against the rationalism of the eighteenth century, bringing into the religious denominations a renewed evangelical fervour. it was an evangelism which advocated an unquestioning acceptance of the Scriptures and a strict adherence to religious teaching from the Bible: it was also an evangelism which engendered a philanthropic concern towards the eradication of poverty and of injustice.

There were many Friends who were active in such movements for reform and so were brought into contact with the evangelical movement. However, this brought into the Society a series of contradictory situations, for many felt that the fervour of evangelism was not for them: other Friends were concerned that too much devotion to philanthropic concerns would displace, instead of complementing, the Quaker way of seeking a spiritual meaning to life through quiet contemplation.

Friends in the past had questioned many statements in the Bible, for the mainspring of Quaker thought had been to search for truth within the heart – the Inner Light – and not to place a reliance upon dogma. However, it was becoming more and more apparent that questions about the state of the Society had to be answered, for it could not be denied that there was not enough serious attention being given to the study of the Bible, nor could it could be ignored that the tradition of plainness of speech and dress was being challenged by each new generation.

There were appeals made by the traditionalists to retain plainness, but the clerks of the Meeting had to continually record that:

> ...too great liberties are taken by divers of our youth both in dress and conversation...that all do not appear so careful in speech, behaviour and apparel....

Many Friends must have felt that the world as they knew it was slipping away from them, whilst others would have been impatient to enter into what seemed to them to be a move towards the future. As the years went by there continued to be a growing division between the two differing trends of thought – the traditional and evangelical – until finally a serious schism developed within the Society, with the separation being more pronounced amongst American Friends. There have been many historical and scholarly studies of this separation within the Society which are available for those Friends and students wishing to examine the issues in depth.

By 1818 Lincolnshire Friends, mindful of a lack of serious Bible study amongst their young people, had appointed Joseph Burtt of Welbourn as the Lincolnshire representative to the British and Foreign Bible Society. However, on 7 October 1824, in Lincoln Meeting House, Lincolnshire Friends came to meet Joseph John Gurney. Joseph John Gurney was an evangelical Quaker and to him it seemed that worship, in the manner of Friends, along with teaching from the Bible with also attention to philanthropic matters, could be welded together – that there need be no division.

Joseph John Gurney was no stranger to Lincolnshire. He visited and corresponded frequently with Jonathan Hutchinson of Gedney. Jonathan Hutchinson (1760–1835) farmed the same pastures and lands as had his great grandfather Richard, the Richard Hutchinson who, from his prison cell in Lincoln Castle in 1680 had shown his concern for the care of his farm. Jonathan Hutchinson was a gentle, kindly man; an able farmer who had a lively and learned mind. His grandson, Jonathan Hutchinson junior, an eminent surgeon of the nineteenth century, writes of the pleasure of the times that he and other young people had spent in his grandfather's company.

Jonathan Hutchinson, senior, had a great understanding of the Bible, as shown by his many letters to Joseph John Gurney. That he was an influence on Joseph John Gurney can be seen by a written statement by Joseph John that:

> ...one hour with him, never failed to be a source of pure pleasure to me; for the sources of his mind were rich, and the glow of religion was over them all. Our close agreement of all points of a religious nature, and on many of a merely intellectual character, was the means of bringing us into a near and easy friendship, which I shall, I believe, always look back upon as one of the choicest privileges of my life...He was, I believe, a man who habitually walked with God.

How the ideas of Joseph John Gurney influenced Lincolnshire Friends cannot be judged, for Friends were well aware of all the points of view within the Society, but after the special visit he made in 1824 Lincolnshire Friends seem to have settled, without undue fervour, into a tempered evangelism whilst being mindful of the advice given in the Epistle from the 1832 Yearly Meeting to seek for the aid of the Holy Spirit in reading the Scriptures:

> And, whilst we fully acknowledge that 'all scripture is given by inspiration of God', a view supported by sound and undeniable rational evidence, let us ever bear in mind, that it is only through faith in Christ Jesus that they are able to make wise unto salvation.

The movement into evangelism brought the Society more visibly into local affairs but it did not increase membership into the Society, and although the Friends in membership were committed to the Quaker way of life, the insistence on plainness began to lessen. Nevertheless, Lincolnshire Friends were prepared to bear the consequences for the non-payment of tithes, and despite the Tithe Commutation Act of 1836, which was supposed to reduce the amount due for church rates, the nett annual amount in Lincolnshire of money paid in fines rose steadily from £208 in 1829 to £500 in 1844 despite the diminishing number of Friends.

Friends were not the only citizens to object to the involuntary payment of tithes and the account below is from the 6 March 1844 edition of the *Lincoln, Rutland and Stamford Mercury*. It shows how the paying of tithes was regarded by the editorial writer of the county newspaper.

> The Church Party first took from Mr Thomas Palian of Gainsborough twelve stone of fine flour and then having triumphed over the passively resisting Quaker the party proceeded the 'divine mission' of exacting support for the steeplehouse and laid hands on property belonging to Mr Simon Maw Bowen...This conduct is drawing down unmitigated censure on the officials...because heretofore the religious scruples of the Quakers have been respected...it is considered a breach of good faith as well as a revival of the rampant spirit of oppression that was rife in the palmy days of church dominancy. After the heavy rate of sixpence in the pound had long been denied by the anti-rate party, a kind of compromise was offered and conceded, whereby twopence and consequently one and a half pence was granted...The anti-rate party, angelically mild, were desirous of avoiding all ill-feeling and putting all antagonism to rest...The present proceedings are an example of the folly of reposing trust in the hands of those who have previously abused it.

There was a steady decrease of membership in all the Lincolnshire Meetings during the first half of the nineteenth century. Jonathan Hutchinson wrote in 1828 that Gedney Meeting 'was much troubled by death' and of the 'low and slipped state of our little church'. At Waddington, the Quaker families which had been there since the beginning of Quakerism had died out or moved away, and Joseph Chantry had kept the Meeting for Worship there alone until his death in 1826 when the Meeting House was closed. The closure of Leake Preparative Meting was in 1830 and followed by the closure of Boston Meeting in 1836. Wainfleet Meeting closed in 1845 after the death of its last remaining member, Thomas Burgess.

In Lincoln Meeting House on 7 December 1834, after much discussion, it was decided to unite Gainsborough Monthly Meeting with Broughton Monthly Meeting and this reduced the Monthly Meetings to two, Broughton & Gainsborough and Spalding & Wainfleet Monthly Meetings. The Friends remaining in Lincolnshire were now regarded as respected citizens and many were contributing towards the prosperity of the county. Joseph Burtt of Welbourn had carefully built up a pedigree herd of Red Shorthorn cattle, although it had not been an easy venture, for after establishing the herd it was nearly destroyed by an unusually severe drought in 1826. Joseph, after much hard work and patience, re-established the herd and he and his sons, with other farmers, were amongst the promoters of the Lincoln Red Shorthorn Society and the Bull Sale. Pedigree stock of Lincoln Red Shorthorn cattle continue to be exported to many parts of the world.

The Lincoln Quaker burial ground, bought by Abraham Morrice in 1668 and where those Early Friends who had died in prison were buried, ceased to be used for burials in 1855. Members of the following families were the last to be buried there in the 1830s and those burials are the evidence that in the early nineteenth century once again there had been some Quakers living in the city. The burials were of the Fieldsends, shoemakers from the parish of St Benedict, the Dennis family, stocking weavers, also of the parish of St Benedict, and the Fountain family, framework knitters, from the parish of St Mary Wigford.

The times were changing – the Reform Bill of 1832 had given the middle classes more political power and had also made it possible for dissenters to enter Parliament. Joseph Pease, a Quaker, had entered as the member for Darlington and John Bright became the member for Durham in 1843.

England had entered into the steam age and the railway came to Lincoln in 1846. Industry was expanding in the city and the population was increasing. Lincoln Meeting House had now stood for over 150 years and, although its fate had often been in the balance, Friends had been reluctant to lose it as their centre for Quakerism. Although there was no Weekly Meeting for Worship in Lincoln, the bills that Friends paid for coal and cleaning indicates that the Meeting House was in regular use, but not always by Friends, as the advertisement below reveals.

The Lincoln, Rutland and Stamford Mercury, 23 December 1836
Infant School, Friends' Meeting House, Newland, Lincoln.

Miss King, grateful for the kind encouragement she has received, and anxious for the future prosperity of the Infant School, begs to return thanks to those who have patronised her, and in recommending her successor, Miss Telfer, to parents that are desirous that their children should enjoy the advantages of an early religious and intellectual education, has the greatest confidence that the result will exceed their utmost expectations.

Miss Telfer, in introducing herself to the friends of Infant Education in Lincoln, trusts the advantages she possesses in having studied in the first establishment of the kind in Edinburgh, will enable her to impart instruction on the most improved plans there adopted. Miss Telfer, in undertaking the important task of cultivating the higher faculties of the infant mind, will by the assiduous attention to the interests of her pupils, endeavour to ensure the approbation of their parents and friends.

The School will reopen on Monday the 9th of January.

Terms. Pupils under 6 years of age, 10 shillings per quarter; above that age 15 shillings; Dancing 10 shillings.

It is pleasant to think of those small children, in their gaiters and muffs and frilled pinafores being brought into the solid old Meeting House by their nursemaids. Perhaps the 'assiduous attention to their infant minds' was not too dull and arduous.

By the middle of the century the Meeting House was showing signs of its age. It was recorded on the 21 September 1854 that:

...the state of this Meeting House as to ventilation and internal arrangements as well as general repair is very imperfect; and it is thought that some improvement may be suitably made....

John Burtt, Arthur Nainby, Joseph Burtt Binyon, Joseph Hopkins and Edward Burtt were desired to consider the matter.

There are no records available of the cost of the improvements but it is known from sketches of the original interior and exterior of the building, thoughtfully made by an unknown Friend in 1855 before the alterations were carried out, that it was decided to block in the front door on the south side and to construct a side door and porch which is in use today. The old fireplace, which had been tended by so many resident Friends and which had warmed so many tired and cold travellers, had been abandoned earlier and a stove had been installed. The women's gallery, long since no longer used exclusively for the women's Business Meetings, was removed in 1855 and the space returned to the garret rooms upstairs. The original structural features of the interior of the Lincoln Meeting House remained unchanged despite the repairs which had been carried out, but changes were about to take place within the Society as it entered a new era and into the start of the third century of Quakerism.

Chapter 9

TOWARDS 'A REASONABLE FAITH'

From the 1850s – the beginning of the third century of Quakerism – it is recorded in the Minutes that there were no Friends and no children requiring help. The occupations of Friends were still those of farmers, shopkeepers and craftsmen and, as with Friends nationally, their interests and their businesses were prosperous and expanding. However, English Friends had now to adjust to the fact that there was an urgent need for a revision of the Rules of Discipline for the Society, for from a movement that had numbered in England, as far as could be judged, approximately 60,000 Friends in the seventeenth century, there was now a membership of less than 15,000. In Lincolnshire, in the seventeenth century, the Reverend Samuel Wesley, father of John Wesley, had reported that in his parish of Epworth, in the Isle of Axholme, there had been 40 Quakers, whereas during the latter half of the nineteenth century, in the whole county of Lincolnshire there were only 70 or 80 Friends, and with Meetings for Worship being held only in Brant Broughton, Gainsborough and Spalding.

Over a hundred years had gone by since Lincolnshire Friends had, in 1744, returned to Yearly Meeting their own recommendation that no alteration should be made to the marriage regulations, but in 1856 they were required again to give thought to a proposal from Yorkshire Quarterly Meeting that marriage to a non-Friend should not be a matter for disownment. In 1858 Charles Burtt, Thomas Spencer, John Massey and Proctor Hutchinson were desired by Lincolnshire Monthly Meeting to attend a conference at which the whole matter of the regulation of marriage was to be discussed. The outcome of that conference was that by 1859 it was accepted that marriage to a non-Friend need not bring about automatic disownment.

Again there seems to have been reluctance on the part of some of the older Friends in Lincolnshire to accept this part of the ruling on marriage, and they continued to oppose it. At a Gainsborough Monthly Meeting in February 1861, young Cornelius Burtt defiantly announced that he would retain his membership despite his marriage outside of the Society, and would continue to attend Meetings for Worship 'even if disowned'. His declaration would have been applauded with vigour by that independently minded Friend of the seventeenth century, Martin Mason.

In 1861, retaining plainness of dress became optional and it was announced that there was to be a revision of the Rules of Discipline. The marriage of Cornelius Burtt was followed by several marriages to non-Friends by other young Lincolnshire Friends and the fact that they remained in the Society was to prove to be a blessing because it was they who were to become the stalwarts or the 'weighty Friends' of the future, who would maintain Quakerism in Lincolnshire through the remainder of the nineteenth century and therefore on to what is now the progressive twentieth-century Society of Friends.

Despite the small numbers of Friends, the 1860s were to be a busy time for Lincolnshire Friends as the scope of humanitarian interests widened. Also there was a new Meeting House to be built! At a time when more Meeting Houses in the county, such as Beckingham and Winteringham, were being closed and sold it seems a strange contradiction that a new Meeting House was required. However,

Bronze silk dress of c. 1854. This dress was once in the Burtt family and was photographed in Gainsborough meeting house. The style and fabric reflect ordinary restrained dress, which many Quakers were now wearing. The photograph was taken and lent by Norma Braithwaite.

Sturton Meeting House is an excellent example of what had been happening over the last hundred years, that is the continuous fluctuation of the need, or otherwise, for a Meeting House. It also shows how quickly change can be brought about in a community through economic pressures, migration and the dying out of families.

Sturton by Stow is a village situated in West Lindsey, half way between Lincoln and Gainsborough, and is in the midst of pleasant Lincolnshire farming land. At that time there was a community of Quakers living in Sturton and nearby villages. They were mostly farmers, who worshipped with the Gainsborough Meeting. Amongst the families there were several Barratt families at Broxholme; there were branches of the Burtt family at Sturton and the Spencers were at Bransby.

The item below, which was taken from the County Year Book of 1851 and written by George Searle Phillips, gives a brief glimpse of the area and of one of the Friends, Thomas Spencer.

> Sturton is mainly interesting for me from the residence there of my beloved friend Thomas Spencer, a gentleman highly esteemed in the Society of Friends, to which he belongs, and in his own immediate neighbourhood. Most of the adjoining hamlet of Bransby, and several hundred acres of land, are in his possession; and the old house at Bransby is certainly the proper seat of the Spencers, although my old friend has lately resigned it and its dear old hearths and household goods to his eldest son, and now lives, as I said, in a new house, which will not look friendly to me, at Sturton.

It was on the return of that eldest son, James Spencer, from Salem in Massachusetts with his wife and five young daughters that it was considered that those Sturton Friends and their families and their servants were now of a sufficient number to have a Meeting House of their own and so, on land given by Joseph Burtt, a Meeting House and stable, with a burial ground behind, was built for £242.17s.03d. The Meeting House was opened on 2 March 1862 and Meetings for Worship began to be held at Sturton. Abigail, the young wife of James Spencer, was the first clerk of Sturton Meeting.

A new Meeting House was also built at Brigg and both Meeting Houses lessened the length of journeys made by Friends to Gainsborough Meeting, which of course meant that Gainsborough Meeting which had remained well attended and had withstood all the tribulations of the past centuries, was then depleted of numbers of its Friends.

The amount of contributions made by Friends towards humanitarian concerns mounted. Apart from the local and national concerns the aftermath of the Napoleonic Wars had left long-lasting destitution in Europe, and a committee was set up for the 'Relieving of the Distressed Inhabitants of Germany'. The Irish Famine in the 1840s became of great concern to Friends and help was sent, including gifts of tools and seeds for long-term rehabilitation projects.

As each succeeding decade ushered in yet more war and conflict situations, and as each brought new advances in the methods of warfare, Friends pressed for negotiations to take place beween adversaries in an effort to lessen the causes of war. They aimed to aid the victims of war and to work towards reconciliation and recovery after the conflict.

The 1850s had ushered in the Crimean War. There was, in the 1860s during the American Civil War, a great need for help to be sent to Friends in North Carolina and for financial help for fugitive and freed slaves. When the Franco-Prussian War occurred in 1870 Friends had gained much experience of the after-effects of war, and the Friends War Victims Relief Committee was established. In the Lincolnshire Meetings the issues were well debated and utmost support to the various initiatives was given.

Distraints for the non-payment of tithes and church rates were still being imposed. Examples for the year 1872 are given below:

| From Thomas Spencer | Two fat cows for a demand of £34.14.06 |
| From James Spencer | Two fat beasts for a demand of £42.10.00 |

By 1872 the Monthly Meetings of Broughton, Gainsborough and Spalding were united under one Monthly Meeting for Lincolnshire and Nottinghamshire, Derbyshire and Lincolnshire Monthly Meetings were to meet jointly for Quarterly Business Meetings.

Despite the decreasing membership, Friends had been from the middle of the century, throughout the country, involved in the Adult Education movement and later in Friends' Institutes. The general aim of the lectures and classes was to impart knowledge in the belief that 'the end of all study is the discovery of truth'. It was to be a time for changing ideas as those who attended the lectures learnt about and discussed such works as those of Karl Marx, of Disraeli who had spoken of the country being divided into 'two nations', and of those writers who put forward ideas for the improvement of the social conditions and employment of the working classes. There was also a strong concern by the various religious bodies about the Darwinian theory of evolution and the questions it raised about nature, mankind and the Bible.

The total membership of the Lincolnshire Meetings numbered between 60 and 70 Friends. In Spalding the Dalrymple-Hall family, the Hayes, Hursts, the Masseys and the Hutchinsons kept the Spalding Meeting open and kept the various issues about peace, and issues that required governmental reform, before the public, as did the members of Gainsborough Meeting, the Thompson family, August Marshall and his sons and their families, and the Smith family. At Broughton, members of the Burtt family, the Robson family and the Davys continued to devote much time and effort to that Meeting.

By 1874 the new Sturton Meeting had begun to enter into its closing stages despite there being such a hope for its future: the families had been large and with many young children, but it was not long before the new burial ground was in use. James Spencer was the keeper of the Register and in the space of a few years he had to record first the death of his parents, then of his wife and then of two of his young daughters. Other families moved away for economic reasons and one family emigrated to America, and so it was that within 17 years of opening Sturton Meeting House was closed, although there were a few Friends still living in Sturton. It was a sad end to Sturton Meeting after so short a time but, although it was not realised at the time, from its end there was to emerge a new beginning for Lincoln Meeting and for Lincolnshire Quakerism.

The revival happened quietly enough at first, with Donald Erskine taking up residence in the city of Lincoln. He was the first Friend for 40 years to live within the city boundary and he continued alone until in 1884 Stephen Gravely came from Darlington to live in Lincoln. It is the coming of Stephen Gravely that marks the beginning of the return of Quakerism into the city of Lincoln.

Stephen Gravely was a birthright Friend, educated at Ackworth School. He was gentle, courteous and kindly. He had come to take up a position as a departmental manager at the then largest store in Lincoln, Mawer and Collingham. It nearly came about that Stephen would not have had a Meeting House to worship in, for there were plans afoot in the city for street improvements, and an offer had been made by the Mayor and Corporation to purchase Lincoln Meeting House and burial ground in order to widen the nearby roadway. Fortunately the Corporation considered the price of £750 to be too much and a strip of land only was sold to the Corporation for £10.

In 1885 James Spencer and his daughters Lydia, aged 25, and Mary, then aged 24 years, moved into Lincoln and soon the Meeting was beginning to attract new members. Lydia died the following year and Mary, although of a frail constitution herself, began to give support to or to initiate classes for adult education, Bible classes and a Sunday School for children living in the area around the Meeting House. Mary generated enthusiasm and encouragement, and soon Lincoln Meeting House was once again resounding with activity during the day and the evenings, and keeping busy the resident Friends, Charlotte and Christopher Daubney.

Mary was particularly active in bringing the subject of 'peace' to the attention of the public, and it is recorded in the Minutes that 'she was a powerful speaker', and she quickly initiated the founding of the Lincoln branch of the 'Peace Association'. Mary's determination seemed boundless, but mention must be made that quietly and cheerfully in the background, taking care of the day to day domestic details, there was Mary's housekeeper, Betsy Horton and her husband William. A 'weighty' Friend of today, Nigel Ingram, when he was a young Friend, knew Betsy in her declining years, and saw her as a serene and contented elderly Friend.

The other Lincolnshire Meetings in the county had already initiated similar concerns in their own areas and Friends were, with other denominations, working in the community on projects not necessarily connected with the Quaker form of worship – the Meeting Houses were open to all.

There was no longer any separation from their neighbours by dress. The last Friends to wear the Quaker plainness of dress had been Joseph Burtt of Fulbeck and his wife Mary. Joseph died in 1884 aged 91 years.

In Lincoln, for the benefit of those families on low incomes in the area near to the Meeting House, Mary Spencer started a Mothers' Meeting which ran a thrift club and this enabled the mothers to save for clothes and shoes for the children and to help during times of sickness and unemployment. There were many public meetings arranged on behalf of the Temperance Union, and the abolition of slavery was still an important issue. Friends were also concerned about conditions in the British colonies, and in 1887 Lincolnshire Friends sent the following rather strongly worded letter to the Prime Minister:

The Most Noble the Marquis of Salisbury, the Prime Minister and

Secretary for Foreign Affairs, and the other members of Her Majesty's Government.

The Memorial of Broughton, Gainsborough and Spalding Monthly Meeting of the Religious Society of Friends respectfully showeth that your memoralists regard with indignation and shame the system of regulated prostitution which has been introduced by British authority into the Indian Empire and various Crown Colonies and Dependencies .... And, whereas such a system must inevitably be antagonistic to all the work of Christian Missions which the Churches of Great Britain so strenuously support.

Lincoln Meeting was made a Preparative Meeting and on 19 June 1885 Stephen Gravely was appointed Clerk. The first decision of the Meeting was to hold Gospel Mission Meetings on Sunday evenings, and these began to attract large audiences. Lincoln Meeting had entered into what was to be a long uninterrupted period of intense activity.

It was reported that all the classes that had been started were well attended and the Band of Hope had 100 members. Theodore and Jessie Burtt had gone to the island of Pemba in the Indian Ocean to work for the betterment and resettlement of freed slaves and their reports and those of other Mission workers from India, China and Ceylon attracted large audiences. Famine and hardship appeals were organised and on the subject of war numerous pamphlets were distributed and public meetings held in the city.

Social gatherings, with music, recitations and lantern slides were now held in Lincoln Meeting House. There were teas and picnics held for the Sunday School children and for many years it was an annual summer event for Lincolnshire Friends to assemble at Sturton and picnic on land that belonged to a Friend living at Sturton. Friends journeyed there by various means: on foot for some, with the children riding on a haycart; others from farther afield came by train to Stow Park and then walked to Sturton, whilst many of the young Friends, dashingly, went by bicycle. The Minutes which record these days evoke for the reader a memory of a leisurely time that has long gone. The trains no longer stop at Stow Park and the road to Sturton is now a busy highway, but in those days it was a country road – the hedges high and interwoven with wild roses, brambles and sloe trees; the verges dotted with wild flowers and behind the hedges the breathy sighs of cattle grazing in the fields. Another annual outing that was enjoyed was a trip by train, in conjunction with the Band of Hope group, to a picnic at Thorpe-on-the-Hill. After many of these teas, picnics and social outings a special mention was recorded in the Minutes about how well behaved the children had been 'despite there being up to 140 children present at the event'.

There had been great changes in attitudes within the Society during the past 40 to 50 years. The worry occasioned by a decreasing membership had caused many Friends to wish for a thorough review of all aspects of Quakerism and for preparations for its future. In 1886 Lincolnshire Friends, in common with Friends throughout the Society, read with interest a book entitled *A Reasonable Faith*. It had been compiled by William Pollard, Francis Frith and William E. Turner. The book was an argument for a liberal theology:

> Every article of religious faith must be in harmony with sound reason and common sense; otherwise it becomes a mere superstition. The teachings of true religion never contradict the best exercise of the intellectual faculty, however much they may transcend, or supplement, its intuitions.

By the 1890s the evangelical movement had become less prominent in the Society and it was with expectation that Lincolnshire Friends attended a conference held in Manchester in 1895. The discussions at that conference made clear the trend of thinking and of the ideas of the majority of Friends about Quakerism, the Bible, science, education and the much discussed theory of evolution. A statement was issued which contained, amongst others, the following points:

> ...no need to accept the Hebrew chronology or the Hebrew cosmogony as a necessary part of an all-rounded and infallible word of God...that modern thought, far from being evil, was largely a blessing, that Friends would do well to accept the general principle of evolution, and that the doctrine of the total depravity of the human soul was no part of Quakerism.

It was on this wave of optimism for the future of the Society that Friends entered into the twentieth century.

Chapter 10

FRIENDS OF THE TWENTIETH CENTURY

Towards the end of the nineteenth century Friends had viewed with alarm the signs of a coming conflict between Britain and the Boer settlers in South Africa, and Lincolnshire Friends distributed throughout the county pamphlets urging that a peaceful solution be sought and negotiated. It was recorded in the Minutes:

> In the fact of the present deplorable state of affairs in South Africa we feel that it is well to publicly make clear our position as a Society on the question of war.

The Peace Association organised a public meeting which was presided over jointly by Stephen Gravely, on behalf of Friends, and by John Dickinson, the Chairman of the Peace Association. The excerpt below, from the local newspaper, shows that the meeting was well attended:

> WAR AN ANACHRONISM IN THE TWENTIETH CENTURY
> The Society of Friends which holds as one of its distinctive tenets that – 'All war is contrary to the mind of Jesus Christ' – is represented in Lincoln by a number of earnest and enthusiastic men and women. Last week they issued invitations to various people in the city to meet Mr Frederick Andrews B.A., headmaster of Ackworth School, Yorkshire. A goodly number assembled in the Central Hall. Amongst them were 84 teachers...

There were several families who joined Friends in the Lincolnshire Meetings towards the end of the nineteenth century, amongst them the Smiths, the Butlers, the Nortons and the Birketts in Lincoln and the Barkers, the Lounds, the Pugmires and the Jenkins in Spalding, and they are the link between the Friends of the nineteenth century and the Friends of today. Just as the Early Friends had faced an uncertain future, so these Friends were at the threshold of a new way of life. The questions that Friends were now asking were – 'would the peoples of the world work towards a peaceful world or would the power of modern technology be turned towards new forms of warfare?' The resilience and persistence of those Friends were to be stretched to their limits by the number of concerns which they undertook, the public meetings they organised and the pressures which were to be put upon them by two world wars.

Whilst there continued to be farmers amongst the membership of the Friends, now some of the other occupations ranged from a master mariner to fish merchant: from saddlers and blacksmiths to teachers, grocers, tailors and general dealers: from doctors and dentist to auctioneers, land agents and engineers.

Membership was slowly increasing but it was the extent of the outreach by Friends towards the needs of their communities which was especially notable. Lincoln Meeting House was proving to be too small for the many groups for which it was needed. The children's Sunday School, organised on the George Hamilton Archbald method of grading classes and the teaching of the Scriptures according to age, became even larger and Christopher and Charlotte Daubney, the resident Friends, opened up their rooms for the school. By 1904 it was obvious that something would have to be done but, despite the new members, it was felt that it would be difficult to raise the sum of money necessary for a new Meeting House.

In 1904 there was an epidemic of typhoid in Lincoln. After the epidemic was over the Sanitation Department issued notices to all public meeting halls to make plans to improve their sanitary installations. In 1905, therefore, with much searching of the heart Lincoln Preparative Meeting discussed the situation and decided that the time had come to build an additional Meeting House, whilst still noting 'that if wise judgement was not displayed the Meeting might well be committed to expenditure entailing anxiety and care and create a hindrance to growth and extension'.

So, as it had been in 1689, Friends in 1905 put their trust in the Lord and a building fund was started. It was decided to build a new Meeting House on part of the burial ground behind the old Meeting House. The collection of money was a slow process and in the meantime Friends were called upon to decide how they wished the programme of the large Mission Meetings to develop. Like the Sunday School the Mission Meetings were held in the Meeting House, but since the congregations were of other denominations, a harmonium and hymn books had been provided for the meetings. On occasion Friends had felt that the choice of hymns was not always in keeping with the subsequent ministry. However, Friends were mindful that although they felt no need for hymns, some of the invited congregations valued the singing and there should be a liberty for those to sing if they so wished.

Mary Spencer, indefatigable as always and seeing the possibilities for further outreach, was looking forward to when there would be more accommodation and facilities which could then lead to an expansion of the work that had already been started. She entered into the task of raising money and to the planning of the new Meeting House, and by the summer of 1909 all was going well and it seemed that it would be possible to start building in the spring of 1910. Mary Spencer did not live to see her hopes realised. Always frail, she died suddenly on the 26 September 1909 aged 50 years: her work was done, the organisations she had initiated were established and the building of the Meeting House was assured. Mary Spencer was buried alongside her parents and sisters in the Quaker burial ground at Sturton.

The building of the new Meeting House was started in April 1910 and finished in October 1910. The main room, with a high ceiling and large attractive windows which filled the room with light, measured 35 feet by 25 feet; 130 people could be seated comfortably. Friends had sought to have the structure as up-to-date as possible as far as the sanitary arrangements and the building was concerned. Electric lighting was installed, as was a steam-pipe system of central heating. The old Meeting House had not been forgotten and necessary repairs had been carried out. Altogether, the new building and the repairs to the old building cost £1031.15s.04d.

The new building was soon in full use and a Premises Committee was appointed to supervise the management of the building. They were Hannah Smith, Frank Sewell, Ernest Birkett, Stephen Gravely and Wilfred Joseph Smith. The new Meeting House was opened officially on the 19 October 1910 and presided over by Henry Keymer Burtt, the clerk of Monthly Meeting. There was a ceremony and public tea to which representatives of the local churches and organisations were invited, with Friends from Yearly Meeting and other Meetings. A week of public meetings and lectures had been planned and the following examples give an indication of how in 1910 the local organisations regarded Friends, how they worked with Friends and how they regarded the subject of peace in those pre-1914/18 Great War days.

Dr J. Rendel Harris gave a lecture on 20 October on 'An Early Christian Psalter' and the Chairman was the Reverend George Barrett, President of the Lincoln and District Evangelical Free Church Council. On 21 October there was a public meeting at which John William Graham, Friend and Principal of Dalton

Hall, Manchester, spoke on 'Peace, the Next Conquest for Christianity'. The Chairman was Mr E. Murfin, an ex-Mayor of Lincoln and President of the Lincoln and District Peace Association.

However, in those seemingly hopeful and peaceful days the country was about to be faced in a few short years with a war such as had never been encountered before, and the ideas and hopes about peace by the Friends of the Meetings were to be tested and tried. However, at first all went as planned. The Mission Meetings at Lincoln were well attended, and it was recorded that the 'meetings were sustained and full of spiritual life'.

During the four years before the outbreak of war, Friends were fully occupied with the various activities they had undertaken. Many of the grandchildren of those Lincoln Friends, who steered their Meeting through those early years of the twentieth century, are now dispersed throughout the country or are abroad, and it is for their interest that below are listed some of those grandparents and the organisations for which they campaigned, or for which they raised funds.

Henrietta Haywood	Free Church Council
Katherine, Ernest, and Clarice Birkett	Central Education Committee
Ernest Birkett	Study Circle
Florence, Arthur and Gerald Butler	Yearly Meeting Fund
Hannah and Lucy Norton	Band of Hope
W. J. Smith, Rose Smith and daughters	Friends' Temperance Union and the Sunday School
W. J. Smith	Adult Education and the W.E.A.
William and Betsy Horton	Friends' Home Mission
Christopher and Charlotte Daubney	Extension Committee and Meeting House expenses
Frank and Mary Sewell	Friends' Foreign Mission Appeal
Charles and Lucy Newton	National Institute for the Blind
Percy Hodgetts and John Walton	The Prince of Wales National Relief Fund
Herbert, Alice and Nellie Crookes	Friends' First Day School Assoc and the Building Fund
Mary Ann Peel	Ackworth School
The whole Meeting	Friends' War Victims' Relief Fund
The whole Meeting	The Pemba Industrial Mission
Katherine Birkett	The Peace Association

The Mothers' Meetings were well attended with 73 or so members, with lectures on home nursing and home management. The Sunday School expanded even more once there was extra room in the new Meeting House, and Katherine Birkett undertook to supervise the running of the Sunday School. The Friends, mindful that the country might be plunged into a war, determined that, before then, the children should have as happy a time as they could make for them. A piano was bought for the Sunday School at a cost of £16 and a blue and gold banner was purchased for the yearly Whitsuntide Sunday Schools' procession, and many were the picnics and outings during those last few years before the war. However, by December 1912 there was conflict between the Balkan States and soon Friends were collecting funds and the Mothers' Meeting was making up parcels of food and clothing to send to the war victims.

An escalation to a war affecting most of Europe seemed inevitable, but Friends continued to hold public meetings on the subject of peaceful methods of solving conflict and were urging the Government to work towards negotiation and conciliation between the adversaries right up to the outbreak of the 1914–1918 war. At the outbreak of that war in August, Lincolnshire Friends immediately made an appeal for the safety of the Germans, Hungarians and Austrians and their wives and children who were, at that time, living in Lincoln.

Lincolnshire Friends quickly set in motion plans for the relief of the victims of war and as early as March 1915 they were organising public meetings to put forward plans for when the war could be brought to an end. Katherine Birkett, secretary of the Peace Association, took the risk of imprisonment by personally distributing pamphlets entitled 'War Crisis', an act that could have been construed by the authorities as aiming to lessen recruitment.

The public meetings dealt with subjects such as the futility of war, urging the public to press the Government to work towards a future lasting peace in Europe. The meetings were well attended, and considering that the country was in the grip of war fever, it is notable that membership of the Society increased. In spite of rising membership, attendance at Meetings for Worship decreased, for as the war continued everyone was caught up in attempting to alleviate its consequences. It is also recorded that there was much sickness amongst the population, including Friends.

The public meetings continued throughout the war. Dr Hey Hodgkin spoke at a crowded public meeting – his subject was 'Looking Towards the Dawn', and he urged his listeners to 'prepare for peace and to press forward for a settlement to be made on the right lines and in the Spirit of Christianity'. Theodore Wilson spoke of the mistrust between nations which engendered a 'Harvest of Fear' and F. E. Pollard took as his theme that 'Strife engendered Strife'.

A committee was set up by Friends to assist those who conscientiously objected to enlisting for war because of their religious or humanitarian beliefs. An advertisement stating that this assistance was available was placed in the local press. There was, naturally, adverse criticism of the advertisement, although there were some letters of support as the Society of Friends was not the only body which objected to war as a means of settling international conflict.

Friends worked closely with the 'No Conscription Fellowship' and Stephen Gravely, Ernest and Katherine Birkett, Wilfred J. Smith, Charles Marshall and Henry Burtt, junior, monitored the tribunals set up to judge the appeals submitted by conscientious objectors. They reported that out of 24 appeals, two objectors were granted absolute exemption; two were dismissed from combatant service and the rest of the appeals were dismissed. Friends reported that:

> ...the hearings were out of keeping with the difficulty and the seriousness of the task; the objectors were treated with scant attention by the Court and that offensive remarks were made by the members of the Tribunal (by men that were not likely to be called up) which had to be borne without protest by the objectors....

Arthur Butler was only 14 years old when the war started and as the war continued and the number of casualties became catastrophic his family, as with many families by that time, must have awaited his eighteenth birthday with apprehension. When that time came Arthur Butler opted to go, as so many Friends did, into the Friends Ambulance Unit, and Arthur's application form opposite is an example of what was required from the applicant. Many Friends lost their lives whilst working with the Unit.

As the war neared its end Lincolnshire Friends held meetings to plan for its aftermath. They were concerned that the consumption of alcohol was rising and would continue to rise because of the effects of the war and of the poor social conditions then prevailing, and they united with other equally concerned groups, such as the Trades and Labour Council, to press for the alleviation of the 'crowded state of Lincoln'. Together they put plans forward for new housing at moderate rents and

FRIENDS' AMBULANCE UNIT,

8, WEYMOUTH STREET, LONDON, W. I.

Applicants for either the Ambulance or the General Service Section of this Unit are requested to answer as clearly as they can the following questions:—

FOR OFFICE USE.

1. Name in full and Address *Arthur, William, Henry, Butler, 7 Queen's Crescent, Lincoln.*
   Nationality at Birth *British*

2. Name, Address, and Relationship of *Mrs Butler, 7 Queen's Crescent, Lincoln.* nearest Relative *Mother.*

3. Nationality of both Parents. *Both British.*

4. Age, and Date of Birth *March 5th 1900. 18 years.*

5. Married or Single *Single*

6. Profession or Occupation *Engineer's Apprentice.*

7. Are you a member of the Society of Friends? If so, of what Meeting? If not, what religious organization do you belong to? What connection, if any, have you with the Society of Friends? *Although not a Member at present, I have been connected with the Society of Friends since I was 7. Both my Parents being (Lincoln Meeting) Members.*

8. Were you at a Friends' School, if so, which? *Yes. Ackworth School.*

9. What is your reason for offering your services to the F.A.U. Have you applied to a Tribunal for exemption? If so, state the result, attaching a complete copy of Tribunal's decision *Because I believe it wrong to take life & contrary to the law of God, and wish to take part in the work of Healing. Have not yet presented my appeal to the Tribunal.*

10. Are you strong, have you good health, have you had any illness which would prevent you from undertaking heavy physical work? *I am strong & enjoy good health, and have not had any illness.*

*11. Have you been inoculated against Typhoid? If so, when? If not, are you willing to be? *Have not been inoculated, but am willing to be if necessary.*

°12. Have you been, or are you willing to be, vaccinated? *Have not been vaccinated.*

*13. Are you qualified for a British Red Cross Certificate or a St. John's Certificate? Have you had any training in Ambulance work? *No. None at present.*

14. Have you had any experience in driving or repairing motor cars? *No.*

*15. Can you speak French? *Elementary.*

16. Have you any special qualifications which might be useful? *No.*

"17. Are you prepared to pay the cost of your training and outfit, total roughly £15. If so, to whom should the bill be sent? *Yes. Mrs Florence Butler 7 Queen's Crescent Lincoln.*

*18. Previous service in any Army or Navy *None.*

*19. Previous service in the Zone of the Armies, if any, with dates *None.*

20. State whether you are accustomed to any kind of farm work *No.*

21. State whether you are accustomed to horses *No.*

22. State whether you prefer any special branch of farm work, *i.e.*, milking, care of stock, working with horses, general farm work, care of poultry

Date: *Feb 1, 1918.*

Place: *7 Queen's Crescent Lincoln.*

Signature of Applicant: *A.W.H. Butler.*

Arthur Butler's application for service with the Friends' Ambulance Unit, February 1918. By kind permission of Rose Butler, his sister

101

to be built following the lines of a 'garden city' in regard to sanitation and open spaces.

At the end of the war Lincolnshire Friends organised public meetings and distributed pamphlets putting forward arguments against military training in schools. The pamphlets were signed by educationalists, social workers and men and women prominent in public life.

It is recorded in the Minutes that in the aftermath of the war people were weary and when the well-documented post-war flu epidemic struck there was 'much illness' amongst the population and amongst Friends.

Wilfred Smith, in his capacity as Quaker chaplain to those prisoners held in Lincoln Gaol for their conscientious objection to war, was anxious that they would have the means to enter once again into civilian life. He and his wife Frances gave them help and hospitality, and Frances, knowing the grimness of the conditions they had been under, made sure that there was always warmth and a welcoming fire to greet them when they were released. It was the main concern of Friends now to concentrate on the relieving of the hardships that had been caused by a war of attrition, and the list of humanitarian causes lengthened. There was starvation in Europe, so Friends supported the newly initiated Save the Children Fund as well as the Friends' own 'War Victims' Relief Fund'. It must have seemed that there was plenty of work to be done, but there was a fervent hope that in the future there would be better social conditions and peace for the people of Europe and of Britain.

The Armistice had brought peace but it was to prove to be a short and uneasy peace. After the war the membership of the Lincolnshire Meetings was beginning to show a decline again as elderly Friends died and many of the young Friends – as recorded by Stephen Gravely – '...have gone to new spheres of life and duty...some to follow their careers and others to work abroad for the Friends' Foreign Mission Association'.

The war had placed heavy responsibilities upon the shoulders of young men and women; and the young Friends, who in the past as children had taken part in those pre-war picnics, now took charge of the Sunday School and the adult classes and the duties which had occupied so much of the time of their parents. In Lincoln Meeting Wilfred Smith, Stephen Gravely and Ernest Birkett shared the work of clerk and treasurer; they were now joined by Winifred Smith, the eldest daughter of Wilfred Smith. Wilfred Smith had five daughters and one son and they, with Rose Butler, Doris Dixon and Annie Newton, were to put in much effort in sustaining the Meeting at Lincoln during the difficult years between the end of the First World War and the beginning of the Second World War.

The decade of the 1920s did not bring for many of the population in Britain and in Europe the hoped for improved social conditions. Support was given to the relief agencies which were set up to alleviate the post-war conditions in Europe and the terrible famine conditions in Russia. A rail strike in 1919 was the start of what was to be a time of industrial unrest in Britain.

In 1921 the League of Nations was formed, but from the Lincolnshire Meetings' Minutes it appears that whilst there was a great longing for peace and many organisations were working with that aim in mind, public meetings on peace issues did not always attract the large audiences that had attended such meetings before the war. Nonetheless, a meeting organised by Friends on disarmament in March 1923, with John William Graham speaking on 'What Can Force Do', attracted many people, despite a day of storm and snow.

Graham, Principal of Dalton Hall, Manchester, came again to Lincoln in 1925; the subject of his speech, 'Is There To Be Another Great War?', caused great controversy in Lincoln and many were the letters either in support for, or against, the speech. The points he made were that the failure to cure unemployment in Europe, coupled with inflation, plus the poor social conditions in Germany would eventually lead to war. He feared that there was a trend in Europe that would lead to countries having to choose between fascism or communism and that the ill-conceived decisions made by the leaders of the Allied Nations after the Great War meant that the new frontiers trapped aliens inside them, causing chaos within the various European cultures. He argued that drastic change was necessary in the minds of men. That they must:

...get rid of the showy and well-established institution of war. War was an abomination, a cruelty, and was full of lies: it was a business that knew nothing of morality, nothing of goodness. War should be discredited, as brigandage and marauding had now been discredited.

He ended his speech with a plea to strengthen the League of Nations.

The general industrial unrest continued, and the strike for more pay and better conditions orgainised by the miners in April 1926 led to the General Strike of 1926 which lasted from 3 May to 12 May. From that time and for many years after, Lincolnshire Friends collected funds for the relief of families in distress in the mining areas and for the provision of allotments, seeds and tools for unemployed miners.

The attendance of all religious denominations throughout the country was in further decline and although Friends were active in the community, and the classes held in the Meeting Houses were still well attended, there was no increase in actual membership and little interest was shown by the general public when a Friends Prayer League caravan visited Lincoln and held meetings in St Benedict's Square and in St Martin's Square. It was then decided by Lincoln Friends to hold a series of experimental public discussion groups in the Meeting House to discuss religious and social questions. These meetings proved to be successful inasmuch that they attracted people who thought deeply about such issues and who then attended Quaker meetings and became Members of the Meeting.

In 1929 the western world was shocked by the impact of the collapse of the American stock market. The collapse meant that there was a gloomy start to the 1930s and fears for a severe financial depression in Britain. The fears were all too well founded, and in 1930 the 1689 Meeting House in Lincoln was placed at the disposal of the Workers Education Association so that they could extend their classes for the benefit of the increasing numbers of unemployed workers. There are constant references in the Lincolnshire Minutes about the poverty of the people in some areas of Lincolnshire, and of the abnormal amount of illness in the population, for these were the days before the advent of the modern medicines which were eventually to prove so effective against some infectious diseases: there was also a high incidence of tuberculosis in the population. At a mass meeting, where 500 people were present, it was decided that, in conjunction with the Christian Guild of Social Service, Friends would help to finance further accommodation and materials for the use of the unemployed.

The Friends in Spalding were engaged in similar projects and Kenneth Barker, of Spalding Meeting, remembers well how his parents and other Friends were kept busy organising appeals and events in order to offset the deprivation caused by the economic depression.

At Gainsborough, Sophia Thompson is still remembered with affection by those Gainsborough people, now elderly, who went to the Sunday School she held at the Meeting House and they tell of the times when she, her transport an elderly tricycle, organised help wherever she could in the town. Also at Gainsborough Frank Marshall started schemes to help the elderly. One scheme was of voluntary help by owners of cars to transport patients for treatment at the outpatient departments of hospitals, and another was the opening of a Day Centre at the Meeting House for the elderly. Gainsborough Meeting was greatly strengthened during the 1930s by the memberships of Eileen and Harry Fisher and Ellen and Harold Brace. Harold Brace, drawn to Friends through his interest in the study of local history, became a member of Gainsborough Meeting and devoted many years to collecting and indexing documents of the Lincolnshire Society of

Sophia Thompson on her tricycle. The great-grandaughter of Margaret and John Maw (see p. 72), she was born in 1854 and died in 1945, the last of a family which had lived for 174 years in Gainsborough. Courtesy of Gainsborough Preparative Meeting

Friends.

There were many travelling ministers and speakers who came to Lincolnshire throughout the 1930s. Theodore and Jessie Burtt were still carrying out their work on the Island of Pemba and their visits home were always eagerly awaited. A. Neave Brayshaw visited for the first time in 1930. Friends on leave from India, China and the Far East came and many were the talks they gave at public meetings and in the Meeting Houses in Lincolnshire. H. T. Silcock spoke of his observations on conditions in India and of his meetings with Mahatma Gandhi. Members of the Wigham family came several times to Lincolnshire and spoke about their work in China and other troubled areas.

Cuthbert and Bernard Wigham were members of a family which had been Quaker from the seventeenth century and Dorothy Wigham, a member by marriage of that family and now a member of Spalding Meeting, tells that when the Wigham Friends were on a mission they were always prepared, when coming home on leave, to make their long journeys home even longer by visiting famine or devastated areas and so gaining first-hand knowledge for Friends of what was required in order to alleviate the distress.

From 1933 Friends, along with supporters of the League of Nations and the Peace Pledge Union, viewed with increasing dismay a worsening international situation. Hitler had become Chancellor of Germany and Germany had withdrawn from the League of Nations. Letters were sent to Sir John Simon M.P. and Anthony Eden M.P. expressing a fear by Friends of a possible danger that nations would use a strategy of 'the bombing of cities from the air' in any future conflict.

To the Prime Minister, Ramsay Macdonald, in 1934, a letter was sent urging the Government to lead the world in a bold and definite proposal for disarmament. *The Lincolnshire Chronicle* printed a letter from Friends calling attention to the gravity of the world situation and for the necessity of arousing public opinion. There were a series of 'No More War Movement' meetings held in the Lincolnshire Quaker Meeting Houses.

On the 17 June 1934 Lincoln Friend Albert Tuck, J.P., presided over a well-attended meeting organised by the 'Northern Friends' Peace Board'. The speaker, Robert J. Long, pointed out that war sprang from human passions and therefore could be averted by human effort, and that 800 to 1000 times more money was spent on preparing for war than for furthering the cause of peace. In 1935 the Lincolnshire

Meeting Houses were put at the dispoal of the organisers of the 1935 Peace Ballot Campaign.

Towards the end of 1935 Italy invaded Abyssinia and in 1936 civil war broke out in Spain, and the fears by Friends that wars would be fought from the air was tragically realised.

As international tension increased Friends, such as Lincoln Friend Cyril Harrison who, only 20 years before, had fought in the Great War, and who still suffered pain from the wounds he had sustained in that war, a war that was to have been 'a war to end wars', must have viewed the situation with a deep and foreboding apprehension and with sorrow. The peace organisations continued to hold meetings. Winifred Smith urged Friends to follow a series of programmes on peace which were about to be broadcast by the British Broadcasting Corporation, and Albert Tuck reminded Friends that the League of Nations Association had arranged a series of lectures at the Technical College to coincide with the broadcasts.

The year 1939 started with an appeal from the Meeting for Sufferings for prayers to be said for '...those Jews and non-Aryans suffering persecution and that all realise the cruelty and wickedness of such persecution and that a new spirit may possess the nations...'.

Friends in Lincolnshire throughout that last year of peace continued to support the appeals for help and tried to run their Meetings as normally as possible. On Sunday 3 September 1939 during the Meetings for Worship two letters were read out. The first one was from German Friends, appealing to Friends to give hospitality to homeless German refugees. The other letter was from the Meeting for Sufferings and went thus:

Dear Friends,

We have met together today under the shadow of war and strength and courage have come to us as we have realised the comradeship of each other and of God. We want to share with you, dear Friends, our confidence that we are all in God's keeping. Stand fast in the Faith; quit you like men; be strong. Let us try to live in this spirit and meet with courage all the calls for service which will come to us.

> on behalf of the Meeting for Sufferings
> Arthur J. Eddington
> Clerk

When Friends left their Meetings for Worship it was to hear that Britain was at war with Germany

Chapter 11

A FOURTH CENTURY OF QUAKERISM

The impressions gained from the records of the war years 1939 to 1945 is of Quaker determination to relieve hardship and suffering and to press always for conciliatory moves towards reconciliation at the end of the war.

During the war, for all the population, there were war-time restrictions to be obeyed and new duties concerning the safety of the population to be observed in readiness for the expected air raids.

Friend Joyce James of Lincoln Meeting offered to undertake the aiding of those refugees from the German occupied countries who had arrived in Lincoln. Joyce, a Quaker, was the wife of the Reverend Frederick James, Pastor of the Newland Congregational Church – evidence of the changes that had taken place regarding marriage during the past hundred years within the Society of Friends. Joyce attended the special tribunals regarding the refugees in Lincolnshire and reported that kindness had been shown by the judges in interpreting Home Office regulations about aliens. No internments had been ordered and nearly all the refugees had been declared free to take up employment. At Joyce's suggestion a room in Lincoln Meeting House was offered to the refugees for their use as a meeting room and Friends organised social events to foster friendship and support for the refugees.

The first social gathering held for the refugees was on 11 February 1940 and it was a success despite the difficulties of language. The refugees spoke of their anxieties about what was happening in their own countries and Stephen Gravely was to write after the event, '...those of us who had the privilege of being present will remember the occasion with sadness but with thankfulness'.

Friends again offered their assistance to those who wished to apply for exemption from combatant duties on the grounds of a conscientious objection to killing another fellow human. Young Friend Nigel Ingram was the librarian for Lincoln Meeting but it was a duty he was not to hold for very long. Nigel Ingram and Stanley Goy of Gainsborough Meeting joined the Friends Ambulance Unit and, after a series of intensive courses which covered medical training, the blood transfusion service, cooking, driving and engine maintenance they were eventually to find themselves in Europe – Italy for Stanley and Belgium, Holland and Germany for Nigel.

In 1940 Lincolnshire Friends received appeals for help for Belgian and Dutch refugees and for the victims of air raids in Britain. It was also the year in which food rationing was introduced and the culinary ingenuity of Friends was tested and stretched by the various social events and hospitality they arranged for refugees and to help lighten the gloom of a war situation. The year ended with the news that in 1941 Friend Albert Tuck was to be mayor of the city of Lincoln and the good wishes from Friends were that he, during this most difficult time, '...would be upheld in the discharge of his duties and that the year will be a happy one for his wife and himself in so far as the shadow of war will permit'.

In addition to watching over their own property against fire during air raids Friends drew up a rota of volunteers to protect their Meeting

Wilfred J. Smith,
Lincoln Meeting
d. 1942.
Photo by Sarony,
Scarborough. By
kind permission of
his daughter, Joyce
Pritchard, née Smith

Houses. When in 1942 Gainsborough Meeting House was damaged in an air raid, Friends from the other Meetings immediately went to Gainsborough to offer assistance. It was with regret that Friends were notified by the Ministry of Works that the railings around Lincoln Meeting House, which had been erected at the end of the nineteenth century by Henry Burtt, senior, had to be removed and sent to be melted down for scrap for the war effort.

Wilfred Joseph Smith died in 1942. Over the years he had served as clerk, Treasurer, elder and overseer. He had served as a Quaker chaplain to the prison and had, throughout his life, encouraged and maintained an interest in adult education and he had shared his extensive knowledge of natural history and art with Friends and the Meeting.

By 1943 Friends were making plans towards a time when there would be peace in Europe and were already setting up a post-war committee to give information and help to those wishing to be trained for the relief work that would be necessary in what would be a devastated Europe. Lincolnshire Friends supported the plea that in the event of an Allied victory, unlike after the last war, the German people should be treated fairly and that a whole nation should not be condemned for the crimes of a few. A statement made by Lincolnshire Friends in 1944 was that:

> ...it was futile to deal with actual war apart from its causes...there should be concentration upon cause and prevention and to plan for relief during and after the war. There should be absence of retribution; avoidance of resentment and to work towards world peace.

Albert Tuck, clerk of Lincoln Meeting, had the foresight to attach into the Minutes the programmes for the proposed talks and discussions throughout the year 1944. These discussions were open to the public and the examples given below of some of the subjects give a valuable insight, which the mundane recording of the Minutes does not reveal, into the diversity of the interests of this small group of Lincoln Quakers.

Cyril Harrison gave four talks throughout the year of 1944: he spoke on 'Quakerism and Economic Man' and 'The Problem of Suffering'. Later he posed the question 'Is there Evidence of Immortality' and he initiated a debate on 'Humanism and Christianity'. The subject during December was 'Wenceslas or Dickens' and was presided over by Albert Tuck. Bryan McCarthy dealt with the difficult subject, especially during war time, of 'The Problem of Evil' and later put forward another thought-provoking discussion, 'The Churches and Scientific Discoveries', and a later discussion was 'Is the Sermon on the Mount Practical Politics?' Katherine Birkett's contributions were 'Whittier – the Quaker Poet' and 'The Life of Elisabeth Fry'. Joyce Smith and Winifred Smith dealt with three important questions facing Quakers at that time, which were 'Is Christian Influence Declining?', 'Is Quakerism Fulfilling its Mission?' and 'What is God's Purpose for Us?' Dorothy Ward opened a discussion on 'The Two Powers – the Power of Silence and the Power of Speech'; Ernest Birkett asked the question, 'War – a Product of Civilisation or of Human Nature?' and Frances Smith gave a talk on the work of the Peace Committee which was followed by a discussion of the Quaker Peace Testimony and its implications.

In May 1945 Friends were anticipating the end of hostilities in the war zones of Europe and the Middle East, but Friend Stephen Gravely who had guided and cared for Lincoln Meeting over the past 50 years, was not to know of the actual end of the war. He died on 8 May at the age of 88 years. He had been held in love and respect by Lincolnshire Friends. He had supported, amongst many other Quaker concerns, adult education, classes for first aid, the St John's Ambulance Service and the Lincoln General Dispensary. He had been a founder member of the Lincoln Rotary Club and had held throughout his life an enthusiastic interest in ornithology and botany.

The final end to the war came in August 1945 with the dropping of atomic bombs on the Japanese cities of Hiroshima and Nagasaki and the world had entered into the Atomic and Space Age.

During the immediate years after the end of the war, Lincolnshire Quakers supported relief work in Europe, China and Africa. They were concerned about the welfare of those prisoners of war who were in camps in Lincolnshire. Also, there were many Polish and other Allied servicemen who were unable to go back home and Ernest Birkett arranged for hospitality to be extended by Friends to the prisoners and to the servicemen.

As the decade was brought to a close and Lincolnshire Quakerism entered into the 1950s and into its fourth century, the membership had risen to 136 Friends plus many attenders attracted to the Meetings. These were now being held at Lincoln, Gainsborough, Spalding, Brant Broughton, Grimsby and Scunthorpe.

Friends gave support to the newly formed United Nations Organisation and as the tensions built up between the Soviet Union and the western nations, and because there was a growing concern about the dangers facing the world in a nuclear age, they organised public meetings and debates to disseminate knowledge about the problems. Friends also joined with medical practitioners who were concerned about the medical and genetic effects upon populations from radioactive fallout because of the testing of nuclear bombs. Katherine Birkett, who before the 1914/18 war had distributed in the city pamphlets which had been pointing out that violence led to more violence, a conclusion that had been borne out by the almost inevitable second world war in 1938, was now nearing the age of eighty and she, with Friends, found herself again distributing leaflets explaining the possible dangers.

Lincolnshire Friends supported the Quaker East/West Relations Committee formed to foster friendship between Britain and the Soviet Union and, as post-war crises developed bringing with them the risk of further conflict and danger to the world, so they made the following appeal:

> ...to all that do not share our Christian belief that all war is against the teaching of Christ to consider deeply before allowing our country ever again to use this method of settling disputes...

However, the energies of many Friends had been expended throughout two world wars and during the severe financial depression of the 1930s: there had been deaths amongst the elderly and the upheaval caused by war had meant that many of the younger Friends had moved away into other regions. Friends now faced the fact that the structure of all the Meeting Houses, as with many buildings in the country, especially ancient buildings such as churches, chapels and Meeting Houses, had suffered because of the difficulty of keeping them damp-free and repaired during the war and because of the continued rationing of fuel.

At Lincoln it was Joyce Smith, the youngest daughter of Wilfred Smith, who was now the clerk of the Meeting during the first difficult four years of the 1950s. In 1954 Albert Tuck died; 'his vigorous personality, integrity and services to the city and to his Meeting' were recorded by Friends and he was sorely missed by Lincoln Meeting. By 1958, as the protests by sections of the population increased against the testing of and the proliferation of nuclear bombs by the super powers, many Friends considered deeply the possibility of making some form of protest against the tests, as 'Friends have a special testimony to bear in this respect....'

Spalding Friends at Spalding Meeting House before renovations carried out by Henry and Christine Burtt. This photo was taken in 1963. Courtesy of Spalding Meeting and Kenneth Barker

From the 1960s, for the next two decades, the condition of the Lincolnshire Meeting Houses was a serious problem, except for Spalding Meeting House. Henry and Christine Burtt gave much care and time to the modernisation of Spalding Meeting House and, whilst the elegance of the building was maintained, the building was brought up to modern 1960 standards.

The two Meeting Houses at Lincoln were now of great concern to the Monthly Meeting. It was decided to close the 1910 Meeting House, which had served the Meeting and organisations in the city so well over the years, as it was considered as being too costly to repair at that time. Suggestions to have it demolished were, fortunately, not carried out and, as the condition of the 1689 Meeting House also had greatly deteriorated, the decision was made to concentrate on, as far as possible, repairing the historic 1689 Meeting House.

Nigel Ingram, then clerk of Lincoln Meeting, with the support and hard work of the Friends of the Meeting, was responsible for much of the repairs to the old Meeting House. The repairs, at a cost of £2805.18s.00d, were such that the original character of the building was not changed and one of the differences was that, for ease of cleaning, a parquet floor was laid. Nigel Ingram tells of the continual

113

Some Friends of Lincolnshire Monthly Meeting in 1950 at Gainsborough Meeting House. Courtesy of Gainsborough Meeting

concern felt, and which is still felt by Friends, about a large sycamore tree planted, in a past age, much too near the Meeting House. Many had been the threats and plans to have the tree removed, but when the time came to take up the old wooden-plank flooring to put down the new flooring, it was found that the planks had been placed straight onto an earth floor. Nevertheless, despite being nearly 300 years old, the wood was still dry. The opinion was that the tree was at least keeping the floor free from damp even if the roof had been letting in damp from above. And so the tree stays for the time being, a source of wonder, but also of some apprehension.

In the 1970s both buildings were listed Grade II and it was to be a constant struggle, not only for Lincoln Meeting, but for all the Meetings, and for the new Friends coming into membership to keep the buildings up-to-date with repairs and to conform with the new regulations for public buildings.

By 1970 our Friends Katherine Birkett and Betsy Horton, after a lifetime of service, had died: they had both lived until well into their nineties. They had been young in the Victorian era and had been part not only of changes in the social and cultural life of the country but of changes within the Society of Friends. The Society, whilst retaining the traditional aims of the Early Friends, nevertheless had moved with the times and was understanding of the pressures upon people caused by the modern fast-moving technology of the age. The Society was aware of the increasing anxieties of people, especially of the young, of living under the nuclear threat; it was aware of the increase in the divorce rate and of the rapidly changing social mores of the population, but it was still a Society that people who, searching for answers to the perplexities of this world, could meet with others who were also seekers.

By 1980 the membership was again increasing in Lincolnshire. The occupations of the members were mainly of those of the professional classes, although there were still Friends who were connected with agriculture or horticulture. However, only members of the Burtt family now remain who are descended from the Lincolnshire farming Friends of the seventeenth century. Quakers celebrate for the life of Friends but do not erect memorials to deceased Friends, recognising that Friends give what they can of their love and effort. Nevertheless, perhaps the following obituary by non-Friends in the *Daily Telegraph* of 20.2.1987 for Henry Burtt can be a celebration, not only for the life of Henry Burtt, but also for the lives of all those past Friends who, throughout the centuries, contributed towards the agricultural and economic and social life of Lincolnshire.

> Henry Burtt, who has died aged 94, was a Lincolnshire farmer whose plea at an agricultural meeting in Birmingham for a 'farming Dick Barton' helped give rise to the B.B.C. Radio series, 'The Archers'.
>
> Burtt, at one stage the largest blackcurrant producer in Britain, made a significant contribution to agriculture, especially during the 1939–45 War when there was a need to make every acre count.
>
> In 1944 he was among the founders, and subsequently became President, of the Lincolnshire Seed Growers' Association. Four years later he helped to establish the Lincolnshire Quality Seed Scheme, the forerunner of seed certification all over the world. He was chairman of the National Farmers' Union Seeds Committee from 1952–1973.
>
> Belonging to an old Quaker family, he was a considerable benefactor of the Society of Friends in Lincolnshire, he began his career in agriculture farming in partnership with Jesse Boot, the cash chemist.
>
> Burtt was still actively farming at Dowsby, Lincs. until the age of 91. He was awarded the OBE in 1981.

As the tercentenary of the passing of the Toleration Act of 1689 and of the building of Lincoln Meeting House approached there were hopes that an effort could be made to thoroughly repair, renovate and modernise all the Meeting Houses in Lincolnshire, and Gainsborough Meeting was the first to start the work. The air raid damage done in 1942, which whilst not catastrophic, had eventually aggravated the structural wear and tear on the building and had to be rectified. Much time and labour has been put into the project by Gainsborough Friends with the effect that, whilst the Meeting House presents a warm and welcoming atmosphere, the traditional plainness and character have been kept, and to those early Friends of the seventeenth century, mostly from the Isle of Axholme, the building would still be recognisable as the Meeting House they had had built nearly 300 years ago.

Brant Broughton Meeting House needed extensive repairs which required at least £26,000. Brant Broughton Meeting House, once a barn, is considered by many Friends as a reminder of the early days of Quakerism and of the yeomen Quaker farmers of the area in the past. The Friends of Brant Broughton have been careful to retain the simplicity of the Meeting House. The interior and seating are white, and as the old wooden flooring was found to be still suitable for smoothing down and polishing, it now shines with a warm reflective glow. Thomas and Sarah Robinson who gave the barn 'in love' to Friends at

Interior of the restored Brant Broughton Meeting House. Courtesy of the Brant Broughton Preparative Meeting

the beginning of the 1700s, would have been well pleased with the result.

The two Lincoln Meeting Houses, standing together in the centre of the city, the 1689 Meeting House being a symbol of the passing of the Toleration Act and the 1910 Meeting House being an act of faith by twentieth century Friends, presented to Lincolnshire Monthly Meeting Friends a great problem. There was much potential for the two buildings, but the estimate for the renovation and for the carrying out of essential modernisation, especially to the 1910 building, was to be in the region of £85,000. It seemed an impossible venture. Friends began to think of ways to raise the money. Norman Edwards, treasurer of Lincoln Meeting, who for a long time had been in poor health, nevertheless took on the responsibility for starting a building fund and for making the arrangements for the work to be done; and before his death in March 1987 he knew that the enormous task of renovation had begun. The work was finished during the summer months and by the autumn the Meeting Houses were once again ready for full use.

It was decided to hold a celebration tea as near as possible to the date of the celebration that had been held in 1910. On 10 October 1987 there assembled to celebrate with Friends representatives from all other

Modern Lincolnshire Friends enjoying a day at the seaside

religious denominations, and from local organisations led by the Mayor and the Bishop of Lincoln. It was now hoped that money could be found for Grimsby and Spalding Meeting Houses and that by the tercentenary year, 1989, all the Lincolnshire Meeting Houses would be fully restored.

The membership is increasing in Lincolnshire. Meetings are held in the five Meeting Houses at Lincoln, Brant Broughton, Spalding, Gainsborough and Grimsby, and there are groups of Friends meeting at Sleaford, Boston and Swaby.

It is now 30 years into the fourth century of Quakerism in Lincolnshire. The first century was one of change. Those Early Friends, such as John Whitehead and Abraham Morrice, lived in a century that had come to be known as a time of 'when the world turned upside down', but it can be rightly said that Friends of the late nineteenth and of this century have also lived through rapidly changing times. Customs and the disciplines of the Society of Friends have also changed, but the belief that there is that of God in everyone remains the foundation stone of Quakerism. The following extract from a *Small Treatise* by Lincolnshire Quaker, John Whitehead, written in 1661, which puts clearly the beliefs and aspirations of the Early Friends, is still hopefully aspired to by our twentieth-century Quakers.

> ...by a perpetual covenant are bound to speak truth to their neighbour and keep their word, though to their hurt. Covetousness they deny as idolatry; cruelty, oppression and unclearness they abandon as destructive to the innocent life...And being sensible that the earth is the Lord's and the fullness thereof, and that they are but stewards of the portion he hath given them, they do not use things superfluous, which are destructive to the creation and hurtful to their neighbours....

Lincolnshire Quakers will celebrate the tercentenary of the passing of the Toleration Act in 1989 and the building of Lincoln Meeting House. And, with the celebrations there will be prayers for tolerance between nations and peoples; for peace; for freedom from hunger in the world and for the preservation of the environment of planet Earth

APPENDIX

A Small Treatise by John Whitehead, 1661

This treatise was written in 1661 by John Whitehead, an Early Friend, and one of the first Publishers of Truth. He had been a puritan soldier during the Civil War and was born in Yorkshire but after 1654 he spent the rest of his life as a member of Lincoln Meeting. In the treatise he is writing about Quakers and some of the statements he makes are very much like the pleas of the many environmental and peace groups of this century. In 1661 it would have stood as a complete statement of the concerns and aims of Friends and would have been at all times in the hearts and minds of those early Lincolnshire Friends during the years of persecution.

They are a people that have mourned after God and waited for a Deliverer.... In Spirit they are fervent; in mind staid and fixed; in their purpose to cleave unto the Lord resolute; in sufferings for His name's sake joyful and patient; in trials constant; in the visitation of the Father's love and openings of His life they fear, and their hearts bow before Him.

In discourse they are solid, in gesture grave; in speaking in the name of the Lord reverent.... Being leavened through with love and mercy it is against their very nature to revenge themselves or use carnal weapons to kill, hurt or destroy mankind.... Their dealings are just, their behaviour good.... Their Yea is Yea their Nay is Nay in all things.

They cannot swear at all in any case whatsoever, but by a perpetual covenant are bound to speak truth to their neighbour and keep their word, though to their hurt. Covetousness they deny as idolatry; cruelty, oppression and unclearness they abandon as destructive to the innocent life.... And being sensible that the earth is the Lord's and the fullness thereof, and that they are but stewards of the portion He hath given them, they do not use things superfluous, which are destructive to the creation and hurtful to their neighbours.

But, in apparel they are modest, in meats and drink temperate; that they may have wherewith to give a portion to the afflicted, feed the hungry and cover the naked.... Unwholesome words they are not free to use; nor to men give flattering titles because the fear of God is in them; neither can they bow to the spirit of pride in men, nor stand uncovered before them, as they do when they approach unto God in prayer, because His honour ought not to be given to another.

The customs of the world which are foolish and vain, wherein there is no true service to God nor man, they cannot countenance, nor uphold its invented worships by a conforming thereto.... They are willing to give up all that they may follow the leadings of the life of Christ Jesus their Lord and they do these things in the integrity and simplicity of their hearts towards God, not thinking thereby to merit life or engage his love and favour by what they can do. But, being beloved by the Father and having received life freely, by it they are bound faithfully to serve Him.

John Whitehead, 1661

The purchase of the burial ground at Lincoln, 1669

Relevant details taken from the original deeds

On the second day of May 1669 William Marshall, gentleman of the city of Lincoln, in return for eight pounds of lawful money of England did sell to Abraham Morrice, mercer, a piece of ground near the Pot Market in Newland in the parish of St. Martin, Lincoln. The length being thirty-four yards from north to south. The breadth at the north end being twenty-five yards and twelve yards at the south end.

On the third of May 1669 Abraham Morrice legally turned over the land, in trust, for 600 years to ... those people (called Quakers) as a fit place for burial for those who died as prisoners in Lincoln Castle and Lincoln gaol or those living within five miles of the city at no cost other than the preparation of the grave and that Abraham Morrice or his heirs shall not plant trees or benefit from the land in any way for 600 years...

The Trust was to be held by four lessees until such a time as three lessees had died. The remaining lessee should have the power to appoint four prudent sober-minded people, living in Lincoln or within five miles of the city, therefore passing over to them the remainder of the 600 years of unexpired lease and only reserving for himself the right of burial and to give leave to bury.

On the 10th of August the lessees chosen were:

Vincent Frotheringham	yeoman of Fiskerton
Richard Yeadall	yeoman of Lincoln
Martin Mason	scrivenor of Lincoln
William Hobman	husbandman of Fiskerton

The following members of Lincoln Monthly Meeting witnessed the signing by the trustees:

Henry Symons	tailor of South Hykeham
Samuel Footitt	weaver of Skellingthorpe
Stephen Swinscoll	labourer of Lincoln

Roger Williams	of Lincoln
Mary Cresswell	widow of Bracebridge
Mary White	widow of Fiskerton
Susan Colson	widow of Lincoln
Elisabeth Clarke	spinster of Lincoln
Thomas Walker	of Thorpe
John Mills	physician of Lincoln
Thomas Stevenson	tailor of Lincoln
Francis Cooke	of South Hykeham
Thomas Dunne	tailor
Richard Prigeon	labourer of South Hykeham
Thomas Crane	tailor of South Hykeham

On 28 May 1690, William Hobman appointed the following four new trustees:

Thomas Toynby	yeoman of Waddington
William Bunby	husbandman of Nocton
John Barlow	yeoman of Waddington
John Harvey	bodice maker of Lincoln

18th and 19th century representatives from Monthly Meetings to Quarterly and Yearly Meetings

For the interest of family historians, the following are the names of those eighteenth and nineteenth century Lincolnshire Quakers who were recorded as representatives for their Monthly Meetings to Quarterly and Yearly Meetings.

Eighteenth Century

Lincoln	*Gainsborough*
John Cummins	John Stephenson
Benjamin Heald	William Stephenson
John Driffell	David Nainby
John Smith	John Wressle
Thomas Brown	Joseph Stores
Thomas Raines	James Foster
Joseph Burtt	Jonathan Dent
John Jallands	John Morley
William Massey	John Dent
Joseph Hunt	William Gunn
Robert Massey	Theodore Hopkins

121

John Pidd
William Driffell
Joseph Burtt, junior
Joseph Smith

John Hubberd

Spalding
Henry Hammond
John Massey
Abraham Hutchinson
Joseph Pine
John Boldrum
Thomas Clackston
John Proud
John Massey
Thomas Chantry
Abraham Watty
John Hutchinson
Benjamin Kent
Henry Hawkes
Isaac Theaker

Mumby
Benjamin Cox
John Langley
John Bridge
William Rickitt
Thomas Maw
John Richardson
Thomas Langley
John Petchell

Nineteenth century

Broughton and Gainsborough
Joseph Burtt
John Burtt
Thomas Spencer
Joseph Hopkins
David Nainby
Jonathan Hopkins
William Simmonds
Simon Maw Bowen
William Camm
Thomas Palian
John Massey
William Massey

Spalding and Wainfleet
Proctor Hutchinson
Thomas Burgess
William Kitching
Joseph Burtt Binyon
Thomas Woolley
Charles Burtt
William Powell
John Grey
James Bowden
William Manley
James Neave

Licence of Lincoln Meeting House, 1689

Courtesy of Lincoln Meeting

At the General Quarter Sessions of the Peace of the Lord King and Lady Queen held in the Guildhall of the City of Lincoln on the 11th ? day of February 1689 before Richard Dawson, Mayor of the City aforesaid...

This day in open court a certificate was delivered and signed by Abraham Morrice, Thomas Toynby, John Harvey and John Barlow Junr. setting forth that the place where they intend to meet together for the exercise of their religion (being with Quakers) and the Worship of God is at the new house lately built in Newland near the Pot Market in the Parish of St Martin in the said City and it being requested of the court that the same might be recorded according to an Act of Parliament made in the first year of His Majesty's reign that now therefore it is now ordered by the court that the said certificate shall be recorded in this court and accordingly the same is now recorded and the place of meeting is now permitted and allowed of-

Examined 1st of December
1706.

SOURCES

Books and articles

Braithwaite, W. C. *The beginnings of Quakerism*, with an introduction by Rufus M. Jones. Macmillan & Co., 1912.

Braithwaite, W. C. *The Second Period of Quakerism*. Cambridge University Press, 1955.

Bronner, Edwin B. 'The Other Branch – London Yearly Meeting and the Hicksites from 1827 to 1912'. *Journal of the Friends' Historical Society*, no. 34, n.d. (useful for the Evangelical movement).

Burtt, Mary Bowen. *The Burtts of Lincolnshire*, n.d., published by the author.

Fox, George. The Journal of. Edited by John L. Nickalls. London Yearly Meeting of the Religious Society of Friends, 1952.

Gainsborough Monthly Meeting Minutes 1669 to 1719. Ed. by Harold W. Brace for the Lincoln Record Society. Volumes I, II, III.

Grubb, Edward. 'The Evangelical movement and its impact on the Society of Friends'. A Presidential Address to the Friends' Historical Society 1923. *The Friends' Quarterly Examiner*, 1924.

Hill, Christopher. *The Century of Revolution 1603-1714*, 2nd ed. Thomas Nelson & Sons Ltd, 1980.

Hill, Sir Francis. *A Short History of Lincoln*. Lincoln Civic Trust, 1979.

Hill, Sir Francis. *Tudor and Stuart Lincoln*. Cambridge University Press 1956.

Hutchinson, Jonathan. The letters of. Ed. by his son J. F. Hutchinson. Harvey & Darton, Gracechurch Street, London.

The Lincoln, Rutland and Stamford Mercury.

The Lincolnshire Chronicle.

Mitchell, B. R. and Deane, P., pp. 486, 487–8 in *Abstract of British historical statistics*, 1962, quoted from *The First Industrial Nation* by Peter Mathias. Methuen & Co., 1969.

Punshon, John. *Portrait in Grey*. Quaker Home Service, 1984.

Rogers, Thorold. *A History of Agriculture and Prices 1639–1662*, 7 volumes 1866–1902.

The state of the Church in the reigns of Elizabeth and James. Ed. by C. W. Foster. Publications of the Lincoln Record Society, 1926–

Stonehouse, W. B. *The Isle of Axholme*, History and Topography of the Gainsburgh, 1839.

The *Calendar of State Papers (Domestic) 1646–1698*, a summary of unpublished state papers, is a rich mine of information for the early relationship of the Quakers to government.

Unpublished material

The following documents belonging to the Religious Society of Friends (Quakers) have been consulted, through the courtesy and cooperation of the staff of the Lincolnshire Archives Office and from the Reference Library, Free School Lane, Lincoln, with whom they are deposited. Extracts from the Business Meetings of the Lincolnshire Society of Friends (Quakers) have been taken, as recorded by the clerks of the Meetings.

'The Book of Lincolnshire Records and of Sufferings' from 1654.
Monthly and Quarterly Meetings Minutes from 1668 to 1895.
The Lincolnshire Society of Friends' Registers of Marriages, Births and
    Deaths.
An Index of Quaker names, complied by H. W. Brace.
Wills and Quaker pedigrees, compiled by H. W. Brace.
Details of Deeds and Licences of the Lincolnshire Quaker Meeting Houses
    and Burial Grounds.

Further information was obtained from documents currently held in the Friends' Library at Lincoln Meeting House:

Spalding, Broughton and Gainsborough Preparative Meetings Minutes from
    1895 to 1930.
Lincoln Meeting Preparative Meetings Minutes from 1895 to 1937.
Tabulation Records.

Through the courtesy and help of the staff of The Library of The Society of Friends, Friends House, Euston Road, London, the following letters and documents were made available for examination:

Letter from Robert Craven (Sheriff of Lincoln 1654) to George Fox, 1655.
    MS4 210. 128 Nuttall TR2 81. 157. TR2 675.
Letter to Margaret Fell from William Dewsbury No.74 MS4 133.
Richard Farnworth in Lincolnshire, 1652. 12. MS3 58. TR2 25.
Richard Farnworth, 1652. 34. MS3 53. TR2 23.
Letter from Richard Farnworth to George Fox, 1663. 35 MS3 52. TR2 37.
Letter from Robert Fowler to George Fox, 1656. TR4 171.
Letter from John Killam to Margaret Fell, 1656 MS4 88. TR2 675.
James Nayler in Lincolnshire, February 1654. ARB. MS1 123.
James Nayler in Lincolnshire, October 1656. 265. 325. MS4 213. TR4 171.
Letter from John Whitehead to George Fox, 1659. 500. MS4 178, TR3 861.
Mason, Martin. The Letters and Papers of. The Swarthmore Collection.
Parker, Alexander. An account by, 1654-6. The Swarthmore Papers.

INDEX

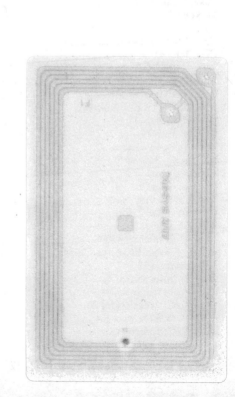